Llewellyn's

2024
Witches'
Companion

A Guide to Contemporary Living

Llewellyn Publications is a registered trademark of Llewellyn Worldwide Ltd.

Art Director: Shira Atakpu
Cover art © Tim Foley
Cover designer: Cassie Willett

Interior illustrations:
Tim Foley: 9, 11, 41, 71, 74, 105, 127, 149, 170, 187, 211, 240, 248
Bri Hermanson: 32, 57, 96, 122, 141, 161, 200, 230
M. Kathryn Thompson: 20, 50, 83, 114, 129, 179, 189, 219

ISBN 978-0-7387-6903-5

Llewellyn Worldwide Ltd. does not participate in, endorse, or have any authority or responsibility concerning private business transactions between our authors and the public.

Any internet references contained in this work are current at publication time, but the publisher cannot guarantee that a specific location will continue to be maintained. Please refer to the publisher's website for links to authors' websites and other sources.

You can order Llewellyn annuals and books from *New Worlds*, Llewellyn's magazine catalog. To request a free copy of the catalog, call toll-free 1-877-NEW-WRLD or visit our website at www.llewellyn.com.

Llewellyn Publications
A Division of Llewellyn Worldwide Ltd.
2143 Wooddale Drive
Woodbury, MN 55125-2989
www.llewellyn.com

Printed in China

Contents

Community Forum

Provocative Opinions on Contemporary Topics

Magical Self-Care

Nurture Your Body, Mind & Spirit

Witchy Living

Day-by-Day Witchcraft

MICHELLE SKYE

This article focuses on the power of the spoken word for spellcraft and manifestation. For many people, the voice is a challenge. They speak either too loudly or not at all. Michelle Skye provides tools to open and regulate the fifth chakra so it spins calmly and with control.

ALISE MARIE

Learn to take what Alise Marie calls the Beauty Break, which is a sacred pause in your otherwise harried, stressful day. This ritual of wellness is truly empowering and can change your entire energy field.

A.C. FISHER ALDAG

In the course of our busy lives, we sometimes find we are disconnected from our natural environment. This article explores ways that even the busiest city dweller can enjoy spiritual practices that connect with nature.

BLAKE OCTAVIAN BLAIR

A lot of emphasis in magical practice is placed on journaling. Adaptability and flexibility can be key to developing a sustainable, long-term divination journaling practice. Blake Octavian Blair details his method here.

DURGADAS ALLON DURIEL

Few topics are more important than how to foster a greater sense of spiritual connectedness and alignment. Discover strategies to cultivate a conscious, sacred relationship with your home and the plants in your home and neighborhood.

Witchcraft Essentials

Practices, Rituals & Spells

The Lunar Calendar

September 2023 to December 2024

Community Forum

Provocative Opinions on Contemporary Topics

Post-Pandemic Witchcraft
Autumn Damiana

The worldwide pandemic that began in 2020 was a cataclysmic event. COVID-19, the virus named after the year it was discovered, wouldn't begin to wreak havoc on the world until the following February, but we are still feeling the results of its destruction years later. It was a completely unexpected event that brought everything from world economies to individuals' everyday lives to a grinding halt. Most people are all too familiar with the loss and devastation caused by the pandemic and may not even realize that there was a silver

lining to it all. But it was there, and it has forever changed how we both view and interact with our world now.

Lessons from the Pandemic

Like any major event, the pandemic changed us on the physical, mental, and spiritual levels. It is important to remember that Witchcraft also operates on these three levels, treating each one as a different plane of existence. Therefore, what we have learned during the pandemic on each of these planes is easily translatable to Witchcraft and should be incorporated into our practice. But what exactly did we learn?

ON THE PHYSICAL LEVEL

We discovered that in quarantine, it was vitally important to mark time through everyday events. It has always been customary to commemorate big life changes, such as a graduation, birthday, wedding, or new baby. However, if you were cut off from your job, family, friends, support system, and even the world around you, celebrating something as simple as showering and getting dressed became common. The pandemic normalized everyone sharing little accomplishments like "half-birthdays" and learning to cook a new dish that your kids would eat, and I think this is something that we should keep doing. It gives us more to talk about, and it just plain makes us happy.

Witchy takeaway: "Being present" in order to live life to the fullest isn't enough anymore. We need to observe and honor every positive individual experience that happens to us, because they help make each of our lives extraordinary and unique.

ON THE MENTAL LEVEL

Introspection was a major theme of the pandemic. Entire societies were forced to slow down, isolate, and spend time alone with their thoughts. This was a very difficult transition for a lot of people, which suggests that there is a large segment of the population that would rather bury their uncomfortable feelings, memories, and even traumas. Mental health became a worldwide focus as people were suddenly faced with the reality of how badly they were in need of rest, relaxation, and self-nurturing. Setting boundaries, developing a good work-life balance, and becoming reacquainted with our inner selves were a few of the most beneficial changes.

Witchy takeaway: Most of us know that a Witch should never attempt ritual or spellwork when they are physically depleted, but what about mentally and emotionally? Since our mental state affects every aspect of our lives, it should be obvious that it would play a major role in how we practice Witchcraft.

Mental health became a worldwide focus as people were suddenly faced with the reality of how badly they were in need of rest, relaxation, and self-nurturing. Setting boundaries, developing a good work-life balance, and becoming reacquainted with our inner selves were a few of the most beneficial changes.

On the Spiritual Level

Spirituality rose dramatically because of COVID-19. In times of crisis, many people turn to or find new faith in their religious pursuits, and the pandemic was no exception. In order to cope with death, loss, isolation, fear, stress, anxiety, frustration, and despair, it is common to engage in spiritual endeavors like meditation, prayer, ritual, the reading of sacred texts, and whatnot. People also suddenly had the time, space, and stillness in their lives to ponder big questions, like what was the significance of their existence, especially in relation to others. Some even found a new connection with Mother Earth and the natural world, since outdoor activities like walking and biking were often the only things anyone was permitted to do outside the house.

Witchy takeaway: It is our responsibility to stay plugged into the interconnected web of the universe in order for our magic to thrive. It is too easy to become disenchanted by mundane routine and monotony, so we must take care to heed the natural cycles of life and include spirituality-motivated activities in our self-care practices.

Citrine Happiness Battery

This spell uses citrine, a stone used to combat fatigue, lack of motivation, stress, and depression. Citrine rarely needs to be cleansed due to its ability to transform negative energy into positive. Since it is the ultimate "good vibes" crystal, it is perfect for celebrating your victories and for giving you a quick magical infusion of happiness when you need it most.

First, find a piece of citrine or citrine jewelry that appeals to you. Cleanse it using any method of your choice, such as smudging, sound, natural running water, etc. Store the citrine wrapped in a piece of white cloth, but keep it readily accessible. Whenever you feel happy, excited, grateful, fulfilled, or content, or are having any kind of positive experience, big or small, hold the citrine in your dominant hand and project your feelings into the stone. Repeat often.

These memories and feelings will remain fixed in the citrine until you are ready to access them. To do this, hold the stone in your nondominant hand. Recall all the positive energy you put into the stone and let it wash over you like a wave. You will feel much improved and may notice physical warmth or even tingling when this process is working properly. Wear the citrine or keep it close to you in a pocket or purse and even those around you will notice your cheerful mood.

When your citrine needs to be cleansed, it won't seem as vibrant and may also feel energetically or even physically heavy. When this happens, simply place the stone in sunlight for an hour or so. The sun's rays will burn away negativity and "reset" the stone so it can be programmed again with your intentions.

Dreamwork to Expose What Is Hidden

We all have dark aspects of ourselves and our lives that we would rather not think about or that we have buried deep in our subconscious mind. However, it is important to be aware of this "shadow self" and to do the work uncovering it so that we can deal with any issues head-on. This can be accomplished through dreamwork, which is great for introspection, for a mental health check, or even for digging deep into your psyche to see if there are old wounds or past events holding you back. It may also enlighten you as to how you feel about your self-worth or your overall place in the world.

Dreamwork requires a lot of practice and patience, but if you are willing to put in the effort, it can be very rewarding. Problems or issues that we hide from ourselves tend to come out in our dreams, especially recurring ones and nightmares. Since the language of dreams is mostly symbolic, dreams themselves can seem nonsensical at times and therefore difficult to interpret. Look at overall themes and pay close attention to how the dream makes you feel. Don't *think* too hard about the meaning of the dream or you will miss the point.

It is also important to mention that dreamwork is best accomplished without the use of mind-altering substances (like drugs, alcohol, or caffeine), because these interfere with normal sleep cycles and can cause a person to skip the REM stage of sleep, which is when we do most of our dreaming. Do your best to abstain from these for at least a full day before your dreamwork. If you have trouble remembering your dreams, try this dream ritual before you go to sleep.

Dream Meditation

One hour before bed, make a warm cup of strawberry milk by blending a half cup of chopped strawberries with a cup of dairy or plant milk until smooth. Add honey to taste and heat the mixture slowly in a small saucepan until it reaches the desired temperature (do not boil). Drink the milk and prepare for bed as normal. Turn off all unnecessary light sources, including screens.

Sit or lie somewhere comfortable, preferably in your bed. Close your eyes and breathe deeply for a few minutes to relax. Then ask the question "What am I hiding from myself?" If you are aurally inclined, whisper it to yourself like a chant. If you are a more visual person, imagine writing it out and focus on seeing it in print. However you ask it, the point is to "program" your mind so that it will dream answers to the question when you fall asleep.

Dreamwork is best accomplished without the use of mind-altering substances (like drugs, alcohol, or caffeine), because these interfere with normal sleep cycles and can cause a person to skip the REM stage of sleep, which is when we do most of our dreaming.

Keep a pad of paper or journal and a pen nearby when you go to bed. Anytime you wake, you must jot down information about your dreams or you will likely forget it. Instead of writing a narrative, focus on key bullet points or even draw pictures, because capturing the essence of the dream is more important than focusing on individual details. Be persistent! Repetition is important as you train your brain to respond to your dream questions, so practice this dream meditation as often as you can until you get the answers you are seeking.

Divining by Seed Germination

During the pandemic, many people adopted new hobbies like knitting, making bread, and gardening. Time spent at home soul-searching also led many to discover that they not only wanted to try or learn new things but also wanted to return to a different life than they led before. If you are wondering how to "grow" your next major project, this divination is for you. It will help clarify which of your enterprises you should put the most effort into.

You will need an egg carton, some potting soil, a packet of sunflower seeds, a permanent marker, and a spray bottle. Come up with a list of things that you want to work toward in your life. Maybe you want to spend more quality time with your family, save up for a vacation, or learn how to play a sport. You can have up to twelve self-improvement projects on your list, since an egg carton has twelve cups in it.

Place a heaping tablespoon or two of soil into each egg cup, pressing lightly. Use the marker to write each goal on the section of the inside of the lid that corresponds with each cup. Next, poke a small hole in the middle of the soil in each cup with your finger.

Now get ready to visualize. As you pick up one seed, state your first goal aloud or in your mind and imagine yourself achieving that goal. Place the seed inside the hole and cover it with soil, then do the same with the next seed until they have all been planted. Spritz all the cups liberally with water as you say this rhyme or a similar one you make up yourself:

Soil dark and soil rich,
Water fresh and water clear,
Fertile seed that I bewitch,
Grow the wish I hold most dear.

Repeat the rhyme every time you water your seeds, and make sure to keep everything moist. (You may want to place the carton on a tray if it becomes soggy.) The first seed to sprout will indicate what you need most at this moment in your life and therefore what you should work on. Plant the seed outside when it is warm enough, and if you are lucky, it will grow into a big, beautiful sunflower that will provide seeds for you to try the divination again next year.

Autumn Damiana *is an author, artist, crafter, and amateur photographer. She is a solitary eclectic Cottage Witch who has been following her Pagan path for almost two decades and is a regular contributor to the Llewellyn annuals. Along with writing and making art, Autumn has earned degrees in both sociology and early childhood education. She lives with her husband and doggie familiar in the beautiful San Francisco Bay Area. Visit her online at autumndamiana.com.*

Illustrator: Tim Foley

Cash in the Cauldron: Making Money with Spiritual Services & Goods

Lupa

I have been Pagan since 1996, and even in my early days I noticed there were certain debates that would pop up with some regularity in the community. Sometimes it would be arguments over definitions, like whether Wicca counted as "witchcraft" or not; or there might be practical disagreements, like whether the wand and athame are supposed to represent east and south, respectively, or vice versa.

But some of the most vehemently argued topics were those on ethics, in no small part because the feeling of being

right or wrong can ignite some pretty strong emotions. And it's not just about individual decisions, but about the character of an entire spiritual movement. Since it's impossible to get everyone to agree on much of anything, many of the most contentious issues have had a habit of rising back to the surface pretty frequently.

One of those hot buttons is whether it's okay to charge money for spiritual products and services. At one end you have people who think that anything can have a price tag attached to it if you present it correctly, regardless of the impact. At the other extreme are those who feel that anything that is even remotely spiritual in nature—including handmade art, books, etc.—should never be cheapened by being exchanged for money.

Most of us fall somewhere in the middle. I'm of the opinion that unless it is something stolen from another person or culture (and especially if misrepresented as genuine) or is otherwise acquired in illegal or unethical ways, then it's fair game. (That then leads us into debates of ethics, like whether it's ethical to buy and sell crystals that were mined in environmentally damaging ways. But that's a whole different article in and of itself.) This is especially true if it's something that you yourself have written, painted, sculpted, or otherwise created. If you (and whatever gods and spirits you work with) are okay with you making money off your spiritual work, then I have no argument with you.

So let's say there's something you want to monetize, like divination, handcrafted magical tools, or that book manuscript you've been working on for years. Once it passes your ethics test, then you need to figure out whether you have the practical ability to sell it. First and foremost, you need to decide whether you have the time, energy, and other resources to put into this endeavor. However much of those you think it will take, double it at least—or triple it if you want to be extra safe. You aren't just going to need to focus on whatever product or service you'll be offering, but also websites and other online sales, social media and other promotion, in-person events if applicable, business licenses and insurance, and more supplies than you probably think you need. Don't forget to factor in the physical space you may need for supplies and tools, along with whatever financial investment you'll need to put toward them.

Let me make this clear: it is totally fine to start on a smaller scale. Don't have the time to leap right into full-time self-employment? That's okay! Lots of us started as hobbyists/casual practitioners. Don't have the funds to do every single thing you want to try? No problem. Just pick one or two that are within your budget and see if you can cultivate them into something bigger over time. Limited by energy, physical ability, or health challenges? Work within your limits, and don't feel that you have to push yourself harder than everyone else to prove yourself. Whatever you are realistically able to accomplish while honoring your boundaries is more than enough.

Now let's get into some specific areas that you're going to want to consider in more detail.

Market Research

You have an idea for a product or service, but you need to figure out where the demand is going to come from. Maybe you already have a good idea of who's going to be interested in what you have. You could be focusing on a particular path or tradition (like Wicca or Druidry), a demographic (such as newbie Pagans, urban practitioners, people seeking alternatives to common ritual tools, etc.), or even an existing fan base (like the people who like the essays or art you post on your social media for fun).

If you aren't sure who your target audience is, you need to research what similar products or services are out there and who's buying them. This can take some time, including doing online searches, seeing what's at your local Pagan shops and bookstores, and even polling other Pagans about their favorite artists, authors, shops, etc. If your product or service is going to be limited to your immediate area—for example, offering Tarot readings in person anywhere public transit can take you—then you'll also need to consider who else is already working there.

Which brings up the next consideration: competition. This doesn't have to be a negative thing! The nice thing about the Pagan community getting bigger and more diverse is that there are more niches to be filled. For many people, having the opportunity to work with more than one reader can be an advantage, as it gives them more information. And of course look at how many bibliophiles there are in our community who will happily take any excuse to plunk down more money for new books.

[Competition] doesn't have to be a negative thing! So don't focus on "Well, what have *they* got that I haven't?" Instead, look at it as "What do I offer that's unique compared to what's already on the market?"

So don't focus on "Well, what have *they* got that I haven't?" Instead, look at it as "What do I offer that's unique compared to what's already on the market?" Not only does that help you avoid falling into the trap of "comparison is the thief of joy," but it also helps you to get a better sense of how to present what you'll be selling. (More about that later.)

Setting Up Shop

Now it's time to figure out how people are going to find you and your goods and/or services. Will you be selling in person or online, or both? Most people do a combination of both, especially with the internet being such a crucial tool for communication and promotion. You'll need to decide how much of a web presence you're going to have. Some people have elaborate websites and multiple social media accounts, while others have a Facebook page and that's it. Remember that the more places you can be found online, the more likely it is people will be able to find you, especially on their own.

While social media is an excellent tool for connecting with potential buyers and networking with others, a nicely designed website is still considered the most professional online presence, even if it's fairly simple. Some sales sites like Etsy and Square allow you to build a website connected to your shop and sales. Companies like Wordpress and Wix offer free user-friendly website building platforms. You can even hire a professional web developer to create and maintain your site if you just don't want to do it yourself for whatever reason. Just make sure your website makes it easy for people to find and purchase what you're offering.

If you need an in-person presence as well, explore your options thoroughly. Are you going to stick to primarily Pagan events like festivals, conventions, and Pagan Pride Day? Or will you be branching out into more mundane venues like street fairs and bookstores? Sadly, due to ongoing problems with religious bigotry, the latter may be easier—and safer—in some areas than others. So consider what is an acceptable level of risk for you, especially if you are not fully out of the broom closet.

Be aware that in-person vending can require a lot of infrastructure. At the very least, you're going to need a pop-up tent and a few tables and chairs. If you're like me and you have a lot of varied art, books, and other products, you might end up a needing more specialized apparatus like gridwall and related accessories. Try going to events and seeing what other vendors use for their booths. You can even ask them where they got their display structures.

While you're getting things ready, the subject of pricing is inevitably going to come up. This is another good time to consider what the current market is like, especially in your area. What are other people charging for similar goods and services? How does your level of experience compare with theirs? You may need to lowball your prices a bit if you're still relatively unknown, but don't financially hamstring yourself by giving away too many freebies or not at least factoring costs like materials. Unfortunately I don't have an easier answer to the issue of pricing than that. You're going to need to balance your financial needs with what the market can support and how much demand there is for your work in particular.

I do want to emphasize though that it is absolutely okay to give yourself raises now and then. If your business costs go up or if you see a jump in demand, those are both pretty easy reasons to increase prices. With time and effort come experience, and you deserve to be rewarded for that as well. The cost of living is always rising too, and every minute you put toward your business is one less minute you could be working a day job with a guaranteed paycheck (or resting and relaxing for that matter). So give yourself periodic raises to help pay your bills and build up your business, even if this isn't your primary form of income.

Promotion, Promotion, Promotion

This is the part of the process that trips up a lot of people. Even some of the most creative people out there can struggle with promotion, either because they aren't entirely sure how to get the word out or because they feel uncomfortable "bragging" about their work.

Let's tackle the latter one first. Let me make it clear that if you've ever met a Pagan author, artist, or other business owner, every single one of us has had times when we've doubted ourselves. Even the BNPs (big name Pagans) I know have been there. So if you're feeling unsure about putting yourself out there, you're in excellent company.

I think this reluctance to promote ourselves is partly rooted in being in a society where we're given mixed messages about whether it's okay to stand out or not. On the one hand, we have a lot of "be yourself" support and a greater acceptance overall of diversity (with a lot of work left to go in that regard, of course). But it's a much newer message compared to the more deeply rooted currents of puritanical "don't be proud, don't get above your station, stay humble," and so forth. Add in the fact that some people have been bullied, discouraged, or even abused by peers, family, and others in their lives and it's no wonder so many of us struggle with self-esteem.

> **There's no single right way to dig your way out of that pit of "I'm not good enough." You can do your best to encourage yourself and replace the negative messages in your mind with positive ones…. And of course there's my personal favorite: being driven by sheer spite toward the naysayers.**

There's no single right way to dig your way out of that pit of "I'm not good enough." You can do your best to encourage yourself and replace the negative messages in your mind with positive ones, and ask for support from those around you. Some folks even go to therapy to get help with their impostor syndrome. There's the ever-popular "fake it until you make it," which not only at least lets you get moving forward on your goals but also demonstrates to you that yes, you can in fact do this! And of course there's my personal favorite: being driven by sheer spite toward the naysayers. Feel free to use one or more of these tactics if you think they'll help you work your way over that psychological block.

As for the practicalities of promotion, you're going to need to sort out where you have the largest audience and what you have the time for. When I was first getting started, I promoted everywhere I could. I had multiple blogs and social media accounts and was on several message boards, and I promoted my work on all of them. It was, unsurprisingly, exhausting. And I found over time that the time I spent posting to the bulk of these was better put toward actually making art or writing.

Today, I have one blog and a few social media accounts on which I've built significant audiences over the years, and these are sufficient. I don't think it was a mistake to try as many options as I did. It gave me the opportunity to get the word out and find out which methods were most successful, so I knew where to concentrate my efforts.

Do try to avoid spamming. On social media, it helps to be engaged in your community, so spend some time looking at other people's posts and commenting on them. It could turn into some good conversations, and you just might end up making some friends and connections in the process. Also, avoid promoting your work in inappropriate places. If you're in a Facebook group that is primarily for discussion and no one else seems to be posting anything promotional, don't post about your new book or artwork without at least checking first with the moderators. On the other hand, if someone posts asking for suggestions for Pagan books, art, or other products/services, you can mention your work in the comments if it's a good fit for what they're looking for.

What about paid ads? These can be a good option for some people, though you're usually going to get a better result with Pagan magazines and other publications, or online ads that allow you to target a particular audience. Start small and see if any of these yield results. You might try giving people a discount whenever they mention a particular ad to help you determine how visible it is.

Finally, don't be afraid of freebies. Blog posts are a great way to talk about your work or write about your subject matter. You can include a link to your online shop/website at the end as well. I used to write PDF e-booklets that I distributed for free that included information about my other books as well. While it is important for writers and other creatives to be paid for our work, one free article now and then isn't going to be the end of the world. If a venue with a large enough audience asks you for an unpaid article, don't automatically turn it down. It might just end up being a great way to get your work out to new people. (Don't let them make a habit of getting free work out of you though.)

On Being a Public Figure

There is a price for having a higher profile. It means that you lose anonymity, and more eyes are on you, for good or ill. That means you may need to tailor your outward-facing presence a bit if you don't want to put everything on the table. Not everyone wants to go public with health struggles, for example, and maybe you don't want your entire audience to know that you're having a bad day. Some people keep their public presence strictly professional and on-topic, and that's okay!

Being a public figure can be difficult though, because sometimes you can feel judged for your every move, and some people just don't like attention outside of specific venues like events or classes. If you want to keep your private life locked down, go for it. Just understand that the line between friends and audience can be quite blurry after a while, as your friends know about your work and you can often make new friends among your audience as you go.

On the other hand, you have a certain level of influence as a public figure, and you can use this to good effect by leading by example. There's a reason that so many public figures in the community may speak out against a white supremacist infiltration or discrimination against LGBTQIA+ community members, for example. It shows solidarity, and it allows those public figures to use their platform for some extra good. As Stan Lee wrote in Spider-Man's first appearance, "With great power there must also come—great responsibility!" (*Amazing Fantasy #15*, August 1962).

When to Throw in the Towel

Let's say you've gone for some time without the level of success you'd hoped for. Maybe you're struggling to find the time to keep up with everything or your endeavor isn't even paying for itself. That's the time to consider whether you need to scale things back, try another approach, or let it go entirely. Be realistic with yourself; too much optimism or pessimism can cloud your judgment. If you need to step away for a bit to reconsider or talk to other people about it, you may find the room you need to make a decision.

The other thing to consider is whether you're still enjoying what you do. A lot of people have tried to turn a hobby or spiritual practice into an income stream and found that it just wasn't fun anymore with all the work involved. One of the perks of self-employment is getting to do what you enjoy for a living, and if you're just as miserable with your business as you were in a day job, then you're obviously not getting that benefit.

I do want to emphasize the need for patience. Too many people go into a business endeavor, whether spiritual or otherwise, with big plans and unrealistic expectations. The fact is that most businesses fold within the first few years, and those that succeed usually take years to get to the point of being self-sustaining, never mind being able to pay the everyday bills. Before you decide to call it quits, take a good, long look at what you've been doing and see if there's any way you can recalibrate your scale and pace of work to be easier on yourself or if there's something you can change to make it fun again.

And if the answer is still no, then there's absolutely no shame in deciding to be done. Not every plan goes perfectly, and with any success in life there are usually a bunch of failed attempts. But that doesn't mean the time and effort were wasted. Be proud of yourself for having the courage to try something new, and think about what you learned during the process. Most folks never get out of their comfort zone that much, and you have almost certainly grown as a person. That, to me, is a pretty good sign that something went right.

Fire Up Your Cauldron!

Turning a spiritual craft or practice into a business has its challenges, but for those who have found success it's worth all the work. Just remember to be patient with yourself; no business is going to turn a profit overnight, and you should consider this a marathon rather than a sprint. Don't despair if you find you need to keep a day job for a while as you build up your business on the side. You may find one day that the time is right to make the big step into being self-employed full-time. Best of luck!

Lupa *is an author, artist, and nature-lover in the Pacific Northwest. She has written several books on nature-based paganism and is the creator of the* Tarot of Bones. *More about her work may be found at www.thegreenwolf.com.*

Illustrator: M. Kathryn Thompson

Practicing Witchcraft on Vacation

Ari & Jason Mankey

Vacation comes in a variety of forms. For some people, vacation is a nonstop whirlwind of museums, sacred sites, and stunning vistas. Others prefer a leisurely and relaxed trip far away from their fellow tourists. No matter your style of vacation, Witchcraft can make your next trip extra magickal!

Pre-Vacation

For the two of us, vacation starts long before we step on a plane or get in the car. It starts when we begin planning our next big adventure. Having something

to look forward to, whether it's Stonehenge or Yellowstone National Park, helps us get through the worst workdays. Planning a big trip is like a vacation for the mind, a quick and easy getaway when we want to tune out life's pressures. Thinking about an upcoming vacation long in advance also helps us narrow down what we want to do when visiting a new destination.

Vacations often present a variety of choices, and when we aren't sure exactly how to prioritize stops on a trip, we get out the Tarot cards! A quick Tarot consultation can help determine if we will have more fun going to Universal Studios or Disney World. The cards can also help reveal what stops we are most truly excited about. Would we rather spend our time visiting museums and the art they contain, or would we rather wander around ancient ruins? Most often it's the ruins that call to us.

We also believe that pre-vacation magick and libations are essential to having a good trip. Before leaving the house for an extended period, we like to leave offerings to the spirits and deities who watch over our home (and our cats). No one wants a phone call telling them their house has been vandalized or broken into when they are hundreds of miles away from home. A little wine poured onto the ground in your backyard (or in a nearby bush or patch of grass) can go a long way toward ensuring the favor of your favorite deity!

Though we like being away from home, we always want to return (safe and sound) to it. To ensure that happens and that our luggage arrives when flying, we always do a little magnet magick. For this particular spell, you will need a pair of magnets for every person traveling and a second pair of magnets for every piece of luggage you don't want your airline misplacing. Start by holding one of the pairs of magnets in your hand and saying:

Though far and wide I may roam,
May these magnets bring me home.

Place one of the magnets on a magnetic surface in your home (such as a refrigerator or other appliance) and keep the other one close to you as you travel (in a place such as a pocket or purse).

Now hold the second pair of magnets in your dominant hand and envision your luggage always coming back to you promptly and undamaged. Hold onto that image in your mind while saying:

These two magnets together are bound.
May all return to me safe and sound.

Put one of the magnets in your luggage and keep the other one on your person or in a personal item such as a backpack or purse. Repeat this spell with every piece of luggage you check.

Practicing Witchcraft in Public Spaces

Many of our travels revolve around visiting sacred sites from pagan antiquity. There's something powerful about being in a space where gods such as Dionysus and Athena were once actively and publicly worshipped. The emotion and energy we feel in such places often results in us wanting to engage in some on-the-spot ritual and magick, no matter how many prying eyes surround us! Despite how badly we might want to do ritual, we know that lighting candles or casting a circle with an athame in public are activities that are likely to get us in trouble. Luckily there are always alternatives!

The easiest alternative to doing spellwork in public is to just soak in the ancient energies around you and commit those feelings to memory so they can be utilized later. When we visited the National Archeological Museum in Athens, Greece, we were overcome with emotion while gazing upon a statue of Aphrodite and Pan that we had seen dozens of times before in history and mythology books. Both of us wanted to lavish Pan and Aphrodite with poetry and praise, but to do so would have probably gotten us kicked out of the museum for creating a spectacle. Instead, we just stood there intently, getting as close to the statue as we could and feeling its energy wash over us.

We must have stood rooted in the same spot for about five minutes or so, letting our eyes shift slightly out of focus to hide the fact that we were in a modern museum. Extending our senses a little bit, we could feel the powers of Aphrodite and Pan surround us, transforming a somewhat mundane space into a magickal one. Because we took the time to appreciate and touch the energy around us, we can both easily go back to that moment in time and harness those memories in our practice of the Craft.

It's much easier to experience the energies of a place in a natural space....Outdoors—away from heaters, air conditioners, and the close proximity of our fellow humans—we can truly sense the environment around us and the powers that dwell there.

It's much easier to experience the energies of a place in a natural space. Whether you are at a beach, in a forest, or at the top of a mountain, there's a good chance you can get in touch with the spirits of that area without attracting any attention. Just like at the museum, taking a few moments in silence to soak in the energy of a place works quite well, but outdoors it's much easier to engage all of your senses. Outdoors—away from heaters, air conditioners, and the close proximity of our fellow humans—we can truly sense the environment around us and the powers that dwell there.

Take the time to feel the landscape around you. Raise your head to the sky and see the sun shine down upon you, letting its rays warm your body and soul. Use your hand to trace the lines on the trunk of a tree or touch the surface of a sacred stone where our ancestors worshipped thousands of years ago. Notice the ground under your feet and the energies that arise from it. Take a deep breath and notice the scents of the world around you and the power contained in the air as it fills your lungs. As humans, we love looking at things, but how much do we really see? Take some time to truly observe what's around you and commit it to memory.

In Witchcraft, our relationships are reciprocal. We don't just take from our deities or the places we visit; we do our best to give back to those powers. Offerings when on vacation can be elaborate or simple.

Offerings when on vacation can be elaborate or simple. Water is one of our favorite gifts to leave when visiting outdoor spaces. The spirits of the place we are visiting appreciate it, and so do the trees, plants, and ground sharing space with those spirits!

Water is one of our favorite gifts to leave when visiting outdoor spaces. The spirits of the place we are visiting appreciate it, and so do the trees, plants, and ground sharing space with those spirits! Water is also unobtrusive; even in a crowded spot it's easy enough to "spill" a little water from a water bottle as a thank-you. (We will also sometimes do this with wine when at an outdoor café.)

On big trips we often bring special offerings with us to leave at sacred sites. Those offerings are always natural items and don't contain any plant material that might introduce an invasive species into an environment. On our first trip to Glastonbury Tor, we left a couple of seashells we had collected from one of our local beaches in California. (I wonder what archaeologists will think when they find those shells in a thousand years while excavating at the Tor?) Leaving a bit of California in England always feels like a way to connect two very different places that we both love for different reasons.

Offerings don't have to be physical either. They can simply be offerings of energy. We find that this energy is especially appreciated in areas where the only vibes floating around the place are "tourist energy." Most visitors to the Acropolis in Athens have never worshipped the gods whose temples still stand there (in various states of disrepair, of course, but they are still there), and the result is an area that doesn't feel as spiritually alive as we might wish. But whispering a prayer to Athena or Zeus and sharing a bit of personal power goes a long way toward imbuing such places with spiritual energy once more.

Be a Local!

When visiting Athens in 2018, we sat down with our tour guide, Dimitri, for a late morning cup of coffee and a quick chat. Dimitri was curious why our itinerary had us visiting so many ruins and museums and why we appeared overly bored when stopping at more modern spots. We don't always admit to being Witches with people we don't know, but Dimitri was so easygoing and welcoming that we assumed he wouldn't be bothered by our spiritual activities. After hearing that we practiced Witchcraft, Dimitri nodded his head and confessed to not being very religious, but he also admitted that he occasionally uttered prayers to the goddess Athena! There was something about that revelation that made Athens feel more alive and magickal to us (and Dimitri even cooler!).

Not everyone is comfortable initiating conversations with strangers, but talking to the locals is one of our favorite things to do when traveling. No one knows a place or region better than the people who actually live there! When sitting at bars or coffee shops, we often initiate conversations with the people around us, and have been rewarded for it numerous times. People love to talk about their favorite things, whether that's a bookstore or the perfect spot to view a dazzling sunset. One doesn't have to be a Witch (or pray to Athena) to have a connection with where they live. All sorts of people over the years have guided us to magickal spots.

Not good at talking to people you don't know? There's a lot of great information online, especially when you get away from the big review sites that cater strictly to tourists. (Add the word "local" and the name of your vacation destination to your search queries on the internet and you'll find a whole lot of places that don't normally show up in travel books.) Servers and bartenders are always happy to talk about where they live and are easy to talk to since they want you to be comfortable and have a good experience. (Be sure to give them an extra tip if they provide you with some great ideas!) Just keeping your ears open when out and about will sometimes lead you to adventures off the beaten path.

With Witchcraft and Paganism becoming increasingly popular, there are more opportunities than ever to meet other magickal folks. We love visiting local Witch stores, not just for the books, but for the conversations too! Most shop owners are happy to talk about the local Witch scene (provided they aren't too busy) and share ideas on things to do. Local Witch shops are also a great place to see what's currently popular in a community. Certain places will often have a favorite author or two, perhaps one you've never encountered before.

No Witch shop where you are traveling? Hit a local bookstore and check out their regional offerings. You can usually find location-specific books in big tourist spots devoted to local folklore, hauntings, and other unexplained phenomena. If the place you are visiting has any connection to Witchcraft (modern or ancient), you'll usually find it in these types of books.

It's not necessary to buy souvenirs when on vacation, but we often can't help ourselves. We like to pick up a Yuletide ornament at most places we visit to remind us of our travels and experiences over the years. One of our most prized possessions is a piece of Preseli bluestone, which is the same type of rock as the famous blue stones at Stonehenge. (We purchased our stone from a legitimate shop that had permission to sell such stones. They weren't chips from the rocks at Stonehenge!) Material things, especially natural ones, can connect us to the places we travel to, and come in handy when working magick. We use our blue stone when doing healing spells.

For many of us who practice Witchcraft, it's impossible to ever disconnect fully from the Craft. Small activities can have a powerful impact on your spiritual practice and make your vacation even more memorable. But remember, no matter what you do on vacation, it's your vacation. If you want to spend a few days doing nothing more than sleeping in and sipping margaritas on the beach, there's nothing wrong with that. It's perfectly acceptable to just park your broom and get away from Witchcraft practices for a couple of days.

Ari Mankey has been practicing Witchcraft and creating spells for over twenty years. Away from the Craft, she has devoted her life to medical laboratory science and developing the perfect whisky ice cream. She is a coauthor of The Witch's Book of Spellcraft.

Jason Mankey has written nine books for Llewellyn and is a frequent speaker and teacher at Pagan festivals across North America. He lives in Northern California with his wife, Ari, where they run two local covens. You can follow him on Instagram and Twitter @panmankey.

Illustrator: Bri Hermanson

Right Work: Using Magick to Enhance Social Justice and Charity Work

Emily Carlin

Magic is an amazing tool for improving our lives and the lives of those we care about. This includes improving the conditions of the communities in which we live, work, and play. Of course, magic alone can only go so far. Think of the token "thoughts and prayers" offered by the disconnected whenever tragedy strikes. Those with the ability and will to act choose to donate to charities, do volunteer work, engage in activism, and perform other concrete actions. To maximize our positive impact in the world, we must join

mundane and magical efforts aimed to create a better world. This is right work.

All Things Great and Small: Choosing a Cause

The most important, and often most difficult, choice to make is what cause to support. Unfortunately, the world is full of problems needing our attention, everything from climate change and racial injustice to the state of our local senior center or parks. There are charities ranging from multinational giants to a few concerned citizens meeting in a library meeting room. To wade through the dizzying options and make the best choice, mundane and magical research should be done.

First, we must search within ourselves. Are there causes that call to you? Any that have personal meaning or a connection to your history? While any charitable or social justice work can be enhanced by magic, work with personal meaning will always resonate more deeply and thus be easier to connect with energetically. Keep in mind that your personal cause doesn't have to address the biggest issues of the day. Local work such as preserving a historic home or volunteering at a local school can have a profound impact. Choose something meaningful to you over what's trending on social media.

Once you've chosen a general cause, you'll have to sift through the many organizations engaged in that work. If you have access to the community you're trying to support, ask people what groups are actually helping out and which are less effective. The folks who run food banks, low income childcare facilities, and free clinics know exactly which groups are doing good work. If you don't have direct access to the community, try surveying opinions online. Another helpful bit of mundane research, particularly with large organizations, is to check www.charitywatch.org or other charity rating bodies for red flags. While an organization doesn't need a perfect rating to be worthy of support, a low rating should warrant extra research. Before supporting an organization, make sure it doesn't spend more resources on furnishing its headquarters than on doing the work. Thoroughly researching your options will ensure your efforts don't go to waste.

As a practitioner, you also have the option of using divination to determine which organizations should get your support. If you're overwhelmed with choices, try writing the names of various organizations on a piece of paper or board and using a pendulum to select the best option or give you a yes-no for each choice. If you're only evaluating a few options, consider doing tarot or rune readings for insight into the potential impact of your support. Then you can prioritize the organizations that will make the most of your efforts. Where appropriate, asking the spirits or ancestors of the community for their preferences can provide insight. (For information on how to communicate with spirits, see *Consorting with Spirits* by Jason Miller.)

Divination is particularly helpful if you're having trouble choosing between major causes. Just as with choosing a particular organization, you can brainstorm a list of major causes and use a pendulum to select one. If nothing calls to you personally, consider asking your metaphysical allies (ancestors, deities, and the like) if they have a preference. For example, if you work with dryads, you might choose a reforestation charity. If you work with Hera, you might support an organization that trains doulas in low-income communities. Choosing an organization to support can require some effort on your part, but some mundane research coupled with divination will allow you to be confident in your selection.

Once you've chosen where to lend your support, you must determine what that will look like: work or donation. Everyone has different talents, resources, and mental/emotional capacities that need to be taken into account before giving to others. An artist might create posters or T-shirt designs, a busy office worker might donate funds, and a student might attend protests. Assess your resources and determine what you are comfortable giving. Consider your free time, mental/emotional bandwidth, skills, talents, and budget. Be honest with yourself about your capacity for giving and err on the side of self-care. You'll ultimately contribute more to your chosen cause if you are whole and healthy than if you deplete yourself in the name of others.

Put Your Money Where Your Mouth Is: Enhancing Charitable Donations

One of the easiest ways to support a cause is through donation of funds or goods. As a practitioner, you can infuse your donation with magical energy to maximize its impact. To do so, you must understand what you want to achieve with your donation. Do you have a specific goal, such as restoring a crumbling lighthouse to its original state, or is it more general, such as reducing hunger? Are there boundaries you want to put on your donation, such as it only being used to purchase certain supplies or not going to operating costs? Write out a statement of intent firmly stating your goal and any boundaries to be enforced in order to best attune your energies.

For monetary donations, you can recite an incantation to energize your donation as you write the check, deposit the cash, or enter your information online. For example, you could say:

May informed and skilled hands use these funds to achieve the greatest positive impact for (cause). May this donation facilitate the work of (charity name) as they create positive change. Together we make the world a better place, one step at a time. As I do will, so shall it be.

Similarly, you can create a sigil for your intention and then physically draw it on the check or cash or trace it on your computer or phone screen. (See *Sigil Witchery* by Laura Tempest Zakroff for excellent instructions on sigil creation and use.) Whatever method you use to infuse your donation with your intent, the goal is for that energy to ensure that your money is put to the most effective use possible.

The difference between enchanting donated goods and monetary donations lies in your statement of intention. In addition to clarifying your end goal and boundaries, you have the opportunity to magically enhance the use, and therefore value, of the goods themselves. Are the items being donated for direct use, such as food or tools, or are they going to be sold in fundraising efforts? If the goods are to be used, tune your intention to enhance their utility. For example, enchant food to be more nutritious, raincoats to be more durable, socks to stay warm and dry, etc. If the goods will be used for fundraising, tune your intention to enhance their desirability. This could include glamoring decorations to be more attractive, enchanting bake sale items for longevity, or attracting the attention of the buyer who needs it most.

When enchanting items for donation, particularly items to be used, resist the temptation to add luck or prosperity spells. When giving items for donation, one rarely knows the people who will receive them or what their personal needs may be. For some people a streak of good luck could be just the thing they need, while for others it might discourage growth or allow them to avoid things that are difficult but necessary. General blessings, such as "be well" or "use this for your highest good," are a better option if you feel the need to add magic for the recipients of your items.

Whether you give physical items or monetary donations, the addition of magical intent will maximize their positive impact on your chosen cause.

Sweat Equity: Enhancing Your Labor

Just as we can enchant physical donations, so can we magically enhance our volunteerism. These magical enhancements come in two major categories: support for performing the work and maximizing the results of the work.

Volunteer work can be unglamorous and exhausting. Work like stuffing envelopes, park cleanup, making phone calls, or marching in protests is extremely valuable but can be both physically and emotionally draining. Magically protecting and recharging your energies is an excellent way to maximize your efforts while minimizing burnout. This can be as simple as charging a stone with productive energy to be drawn on while you work. Select an active stone, like citrine or garnet, and place it on the windowsill during a full moon. Allow the moon's energy to charge the stone overnight. Then carry it with you while you volunteer and simply put your hand in your pocket and hold the

Volunteer work can be unglamorous and exhausting.... Magically protecting and recharging your energies is an excellent way to maximize your efforts while minimizing burnout.

stone whenever you need a boost. A more complex but versatile option is to create a charm bag to carry while volunteering. For example, you could use a cotton tea bag containing a small hematite for grounding negative energy, a tiger-eye for energy and motivation, and a few peppermint leaves for cleansing and positivity. The contents of the charm bag can be tuned to best fit your situation and energetic needs.

Another excellent way to add support to your work is to bring enchanted snacks. We all need to eat and refuel our bodies, so why not boost that magically? Add magical intent to foods by reciting an incantation as you prepare them, or hold them in your hands and allow your energy to charge them. Additionally, if you work with metaphysical allies such as ancestors, elementals, or deities, you can petition them for support during your work. Lastly, always take time to ground and center after doing mentally or emotionally taxing work to rebalance your energies. Spending a little extra time to magically support your volunteer work will ensure you are able to do your best.

There are many ways to magically enhance the result of volunteerism, depending on the nature of the work being done. For work that requires personal interaction, like community outreach or phone banking, you could glamor yourself to be more welcoming or persuasive. An option for doing so is to focus on the energy you want to project while forming an energy ball between your hands, then sink the energy ball into your body to be absorbed and align yourself to your intent. This technique can also be used to enhance the performance of skilled work, such as electrical work or lawyering. Simply tune the energies to peak performance of your skill. For example, an attorney doing *pro bono* work for immigrants' rights might raise and tune energy to ensure the accuracy of their research or the persuasiveness of their writing.

For work where something is created, such as making artwork or printing flyers, you can incorporate symbols, color correspondences, or sigils into the final products to align them to your intent. Similarly, you can infuse your intent into any creation by deliberately allowing said intention to flow through you and into your creation. This process works for both physical creations, like T-shirts, and less tangible products, like essays or audio clips. As with magical support, you can also call on appropriate metaphysical allies to lend their energies to augment your creations or skills.

More complex volunteering may involve several types of work and could be best served with multiple methods of magical enhancement. In these cases, try creating your enchantments over time or with the help of others to avoid energetic burnout. You can also prioritize your tasks by difficulty or potential impact and add limited magical energies to only the most challenging or effective ones. Volunteer work takes precious time and effort; magical enhancement helps to ensure the most is made of it.

Do Right Work

We all want to live in a better world. To enhance our contributions to creating that world, we can use our magics to choose where to lend our support, increase the impact of that support, and help us sustain that support. The ideas and techniques here are just a few of the myriad ways you can use your magical skills to augment your work to create a better future. Do as much or as little as is right for you, for any cause, great or small. Every little bit helps.

Emily Carlin is a Witch, writer, teacher, and mediator based in Seattle, Washington. She currently teaches one-on-one online and at in-person events on the West Coast. During her 20+ years of practice, she has published articles on defensive magick, pop culture magick, Santa Muerte, general witchcraft, and more. For more information go to http://www.e-carlin.com.

Illustrator: Tim Foley

Magic and Nature:
The Connection
James Kambos

Magic, Wicca, and Witchcraft are based in nature. These and other earth-based belief systems and religions follow the cycle of the seasons. Many of these traditions utilize natural materials such as soil, plants, water, and other earth-related substances in their practices. They may also utilize the power and phases of the oceans, the sun, the moon, and the planets. There is a deep respect for the link between nature, the Earth, and the food that sustains us. The habits and health of the birds, animals,

and fish that share our planet with us are also part of the magic-nature connection.

Whether you are a Witch living on a farm, a suburban solitary, a village Conjure doctor living by the sea, or a hip city Wiccan, you are connected to the natural world and respond to nature's rhythms.

Understanding the connection between magic and nature will make your magic more powerful. Being truly aware of these connections will help you understand the natural energies that surround us.

I encourage you at some point to go beyond this article to gain a greater understanding of the magic-nature connection. In time you may understand why a spell calls for a specific herb, why you're advised to cast a spell during a certain phase of the moon, or why a spell calls for bottled spring water rather than tap water.

There are many books on the subject of magic and the natural world, so please seek them out. Llewellyn has many books on the subject and is a good place to start.

You may not realize it, but if you're interested in magic, there is a pretty good chance you're already a keen observer of nature. On some level you must be aware of the link between magic and nature.

Think back. Was there a moment in your life that sparked your interest in magic and/or nature?

There was in mine.

The Miracle of the Soil

Much of my childhood was spent on my grandparents' farm. There I was raised to respect the Earth and nature. But on a spring afternoon many years ago, I learned there was magic in something as ordinary as the soil. That was my "moment" when I connected magic and nature.

My grandfather and I were driving to a nearby village to buy groceries. As we drove past a freshly plowed field, my grandfather suddenly pulled the car over and stopped. I couldn't understand why. I mean, it was just some dirt, right?

My grandfather got out of the car and stood at the edge of this field. Hands on hips, he gazed out across the freshly turned soil. As far as you could see, the black rich soil spread out beneath the pale blue spring sky. The scent was earthy and moist. Silently he dragged the heel of his boot across the newly opened earth. Bending down, he picked up a handful of the jet-black soil. He crumbled it and let it fall between his fingers back to the ground. He did this with great respect. For him, this was a spiritual experience.

That's when I saw what he saw and felt what he felt.

For him, this plot of earth, which had been dormant since late fall, was now ready to accept the seeds—the essence of life's beginnings. This soil was ready to begin the magic that would start, once again, the never-ending cycle of nature: birth, growth, and the miracle of the harvest. This cycle has sustained humanity since before recorded history.

In that moment I learned a magical truth: Magic is connected to nature; nature is connected to magic.

Magic is similar to this natural cycle. In magic, we plant a seed—our wish. Next we wait—the period of growth. Then we reap our harvest—when our wish manifests in the physical world.

In magic, we plant a seed—our wish. Next we wait—the period of growth. Then we reap our harvest—when our wish manifests in the physical world.

That long-ago afternoon, as I stood beside my grandfather in a freshly plowed field, I learned a lesson that still guides me today:

Nature is the basis of all magic.

Think about your first magical moment with nature. Perhaps you were with your family when you experienced the power of the ocean as waves pounded a rocky shore. Maybe you felt your connection helping your mother in her garden. Or was it when you heard the first crunch of autumn leaves as you walked to school on an October morning?

No matter how you touched upon that first moment of magic and nature, I bet it still fuels your passion for magic. However, as we get older—and busier—sometimes we lose touch with our connection to nature.

Let's take a look at ways to reconnect with the natural world and its energies. It will help empower your magic and daily life.

Touch the Earth

My moment of realizing the connection between nature and magic, as I've said, was near my grandparents' farm. Most of us today are generations removed from our agrarian roots, and many of us don't have easy access to a farm. But there are ways to touch the Earth, and there are few better ways to connect to magic than by touching soil.

For any Witch or magical person, it's a good idea to keep a dish of soil on your altar. This simple gesture works wonders spiritually.

In the morning, touch the soil, crumble it, smell it. Let its essence become part of your daily devotional. This will awaken your spiritual connection to nature's energies that make magic possible.

Of course if you have a garden or yard, get out in it as much as possible. Having a small plot where you can raise a few vegetables or flowers is a big plus too.

I also know some magical folk who greet each day by kneeling in their backyard early each morning and touching their forehead and palms to the dew on the grass.

Experiment. There are many ways to touch the Earth.

Plants and Trees

Plants and trees were on our planet long before any human walked the Earth. They have known the sun, the stars, and the turning of the seasons longer than any of us. They are steeped in magic and mystery. Since they're rooted in the soil, they're one of our partners in magic and nature.

If you can, keep at least one houseplant. Placing some potted herbs on a porch or terrace would be a great way to connect with nature too. Watch them, water them, and tend them. You'll notice that not only will they respond to your care, but you'll benefit too. As you tend them, notice how more relaxed you feel. Your magical efforts will respond as well.

Take some time to learn about your plants. Then you'll be able to incorporate them into your magic.

Trees are the ancients of our planet. They supply us with oxygen. Needless to say, trees are an important link to magic and spirituality. At Yule, for instance, it's the pine that we bring into our homes as a symbol of hope and life everlasting.

If you don't have a tree of your own, pick one out in a park or a wooded area on public land. Go to it and meditate when you feel the need.

Plants and trees are a huge part of our magical connection to nature!

Seasonal Energies

There was a time when societies celebrated the turning of the Wheel of the Year with great joy and celebrating. These markers on the calendar were important for various reasons. First, and most importantly, these dates marked the planting and harvesting cycles. All food at the time was planted, grown, and harvested by hand. Farmers, their families, or an entire village all helped in the process. Successful planting and harvesting were essential for survival. Early Pagans understood this. From these beliefs, the eight sabbats marking the turning of the year (Ostara, Beltane, Midsummer, Lughnasadh, Mabon, Samhain, Yule, and Imbolc) came to be.

These days led to joyful celebrations. Families, clans, and villages came together to honor the Old Gods and the harvest. It was also a time to visit and catch up. Remnants of these celebrations remain with us in the form of county fairs.

Some Pagans still observe these seasonal markers and days. However, for many, the original meanings behind these celebrations have become diluted or have been forgotten.

To reconnect to these seasonal energies, take some time to honor them with seasonal food and décor. Bake a corn bread at Lughnasadh. Toast Mabon with a glass of wine. Hang some bittersweet on your door at Samhain.

As you eat and decorate, be mindful of where these traditions came from. Also take time to gather some natural decorations yourself. Autumn leaves or pine cones aren't just attractive but can also be used in your spellwork to give your magic a natural boost.

. . . .

No matter if you garden, follow the phases of the moon, or observe the flight path of birds, getting in touch with nature empowers your life and magic.

James Kambos *is a writer from Ohio who writes essays and articles about the folk magic traditions of Appalachia, Greece, and the Near East. He also paints and raises wildflowers. He has a degree in history and geography from Ohio University.*

Illustrator: M. Kathryn Thompson

The Controversial Pagan: Issues of Ethics, Power, and Insensitivity, Part 2

Susan Pesznecker

This essay is a continuation of an article I wrote for *Llewellyn's* 2023 *Witches' Companion*. Let me briefly restate some of the opening bits from that piece:

- We in the Pagan community are just like everyone else; i.e., imperfect. Things happen.

- I use *Pagan* as an umbrella term to describe those who follow non-mainstream belief systems, many of which are rooted in nature and the natural world. I capitalize the word *Pagan* because I feel it represents a host of spiritual practices, even if

they differ slightly. But I don't capitalize words like *coven* or *circle* because there is so much diversity there that it's safer and more equitable to use the common noun expressions.

• Most of us have run into Craft, practice, or interpersonal situations where principled, ethical behavior is in question. Sometimes we find this in others, but—and this is the hard part—we may also find it in ourselves. In either case, we benefit from reminders of how to respond or handle such situations. We may be magical folk, but there's no magic wand that can keep us safe from many of these issues. Rather, it's our common sense and collective strength that will do the trick. Thinking about these circumstances in advance—and honestly evaluating situations that just don't feel right—can be immensely helpful.

Part 1 of this essay touched on secrecy and fair treatment within groups; power-hungry leadership; mistreatment of newbies and novices; fundamentalism and elitism; big name Pagans and fallen idols; and cultural appropriation. In this part 2 sequel, we'll work through a set of new ideas, considering how to deal with each one. I'm going to dive right in to the biggest issue.

Sexual Abuse and Consent in Pagan Practices

We're in the "Me Too" era, where many people are beginning to speak out more freely about unwanted sexual advances, sexual mistreatment, and sexual assault. Even so, and even with increasing openness, these heinous practices continue, and they continue within Pagan circles just as they do within mainstream society. Within Pagan practices, there may even be some situations where sexual advances or even assault are *more* likely to take place.

For example, within some Wiccan covens, sexual ritual and nudity are part of the core practices, as in the Great Rite. Yet not all groups pause to consider the age or maturity of their members or the age range between participants in sexual relations. Legal age for sexual consent varies in the US from state to state. Thirty-four states list sixteen as the age of sexual consent, with others varying between seventeen and eighteen. In some states there's an additional requirement for "age differential" between two parties. This generally translates to a heightened accusation of sexual assault or statutory rape when there is an age difference of four or more years between the two people involved.

Some people take completely different views of sexual "maturity." I knew a coven leader in the Midwest who firmly believed that once a child developed secondary sexual characteristics (in her eyes, this meant body hair and enlarged genitalia in males, and breasts, body hair, and menstruation in females), they were "sexually ready" and should be able to participate in sexual activity. Considering that some children today begin developing these characteristics as early as age seven or eight, I find this point of view terrifying. And let's be honest: even if a sixteen-year-old can legally consent to sexual activity, this doesn't mean they have the emotional maturity to do so. There's plenty of medical-scientific evidence these days showing that adolescent brains don't finish developing until the early or mid-twenties, and until then, judgment, acumen, and self-regulation are incomplete. I have to add that even full-on adults don't always show the best judgment, so why would we be extra-generous in expecting young people to?

What about adults who *unexpectedly* find themselves involved in or witnessing ritual involving sexual activity? If they're prepared for this in advance, they can make the choice to participate or pass.

But in some groups, secrecy is part of the process of unveiling a set of secrets and traditions, and participants may be unaware of what will happen or is expected until a moment of great surprise. In situations like this, peer pressure and the desire to be liked or belong may overwhelm one's sense of privacy, safety, and personal space—especially if they're pressured to continue or, worse, told that failure to do so will make it impossible for them to remain in the group.

Nudity is also common in some groups and practices, where it may be a central part of ritual. Is it appropriate for minors (i.e., children) to be part of an adult skyclad ritual? Such an occurrence could be construed (legally and otherwise) as a kind of child sexual abuse or mistreatment, and that could be true whether or not the child's parents are present. As for adults, many aren't comfortable with public nudity for any number of reasons, and forcing them to participate in nude rituals could be felt as a kind of sexual harassment, emotional cruelty, or even assault.

Speaking of assault, pedophilia, defined as having and expressing sexual feelings toward children, is a serious social crime, and the Pagan culture is not immune. In one example from the past several years, the author of a well-known Pagan novel about the Arthurian myth was found to be helping secure and groom child victims for her pedophile husband. In another, an established Wiccan tradition routinely "prepared" young, underage females for ritual sexual initiation by asking them to use vaginal dilators for several weeks prior to the main event. And then there was the well-known Wiccan high priest who was convicted of multiple counts of possession of child pornography and was also found to have abused his own children sexually for years. These are only a few examples, and while such cases represent a very small percentage of Pagans, it's clear we share these problems with the rest of society. Therefore, we have a clear, ethical responsibility to be alert in such settings and, if we see something questionable happening, to do something.

But what is that "something"? We begin by creating an open climate where people can trust their leaders or elders in a situation and feel they can seek help for sexual mistreatment. That said, a number of people are uncomfortable seeking help or going public with their experiences. This is especially true when the victim is a child or a member of a marginalized group subject to repeated discrimination, e.g., those people who are transgender, nonbinary, and so forth. A climate of openness and safety is essential. If there is suspicion that something has happened, taking the person aside and asking them directly may lead them to talk about an uncomfortable experience. If you have reason to be concerned, you should report those concerns to your local authorities—and do so immediately. The idea of a complaint or concern being pooh-poohed or swept under the proverbial table must be avoided at all costs, for there is no easier way to lose trust.

> **The idea of a complaint or concern being pooh-poohed or swept under the proverbial table must be avoided at all costs, for there is no easier way to lose trust.**

Where children are concerned—and by children, I mean people under age eighteen, a.k.a. legally defined minors in the United States—the situation changes. It's important for every adult to know if they are a mandatory reporter in their state of residence. If you are a mandatory reporter, it means that if you have the tiniest, slightest worry or concern about possible sexual impropriety involving a child, even if it's something you heard secondhand but didn't actually observe, you *must* report it to the authorities. If you don't, you could potentially be held liable if the child is harmed. You don't have to have hard evidence to make a report—but you do have to report. The authorities will then conduct whatever investigation is required. In most or all states, you'll be asked to give your name when reporting. But most or all states will also allow your name to remain anonymous within the report.

How do you find out if you're a mandatory reporter? Yay, internet! Search for your state's information on the subject. In many states, religious figures are mandatory reporters, and this is important, as many Pagan clergy would fall under this umbrella. Ditto for Pagan organizations holding summer gatherings with youth camp aspects or those running Pagan-esque scouting groups.

The Isms: Racism, Genderism (*I know, not a word, but bear with me*), Sexism, and So Forth

Just talking in-depth about these topics alone would require a book-length work. I'm not going to try to go deep with any of them, but I do want to touch on some of the ideas and problems that seem to pop up, often repeatedly.

Racism

No. Just *no*. You know what? We humans are something like 99.9 percent DNA-identical. Our varying appearances tend to be related to our ancient ancestors and how closely they lived to the equator or the polar regions, and then to which genetic traits were passed through migration and such. But our DNA? It's more or less identical. Yet everything about my country, the US, is built on a well-documented structure of historical and implicit racism, with these truths inexorably bleeding into every part of our daily lives, including, sadly, our Pagan practices.

What do you do when racism is an intentional part of a group or practice? It's well known that some public Norse/Heathen groups focus on an exclusively "white" or "European" tradition. These groups will trot out their background information and explain why they do this and why it's okay and what they're trying to accomplish, i.e., "We're not racists—we're just trying to preserve a single culture." Gah! But you know what? This is racist, exclusionary behavior at best, and at worst, it can cloak implied or very real violence and hatred, as in such groups that also serve as a front for white supremacists. These are dangerous examples of discrimination and hatred. My approach is to call them out on the statement because I personally have a zero tolerance approach to overt racism. That said, it's also important to assess the person you're confronting and the risk that they might become angry and aggressive toward you.

A good approach is to say to the person making the [racist] statement, "I'm sorry, but I don't understand what you said [or why you did this]. Can you explain?" This forces them to try and do so, and it typically doesn't go well.

How should you respond when witnessing a clearly racist statement or action within your group or a group activity? A good approach is to say to the person making the statement, "I'm sorry, but I don't understand what you said [or why you did this]. Can you explain?" This forces them to try and do so, and it typically doesn't go well. On the other hand, in the case of someone who is clueless as to the racist nature of their statement or action, this approach may create an "aha" moment that forces them to confront their words and actions and consider them, and this may create an opportunity to learn. Overall, be aware that while it may be hard to change a racist's opinions, I feel that at least identifying the problem becomes something I'm ethically obliged to do, and I hope that by speaking it out loud, all parties will at least hear the words.

It's also important to ensure that our groups and activities are open and welcoming to all. In a syllabus statement for my college students, I tell them that our class is a safe place for everyone, regardless of age, gender, ethnicity, ability, spoken language, mayonnaise-Miracle Whip preference (yes, I really say that), and more. That may sound tongue-in-cheek, but on day one I let the students know I mean it, and I engage them in dialogue as we create a collaborative, shared set of classroom behaviors and understandings. I want them to buy into our shared role in creating a climate of safety and respect.

We can create the same safe environment in our Pagan groups, too. It takes time, open discussion, and a willingness to demonstrate actions that support words. It can be done. It should be done. That said, my comments here are overly simplistic in that we can't expect one simple set of actions to overturn centuries of racial divide—and my comments here barely scratch the surface. There is much work to do, and with every gesture and word, we take a step forward. In addition to collective work, we also have an obligation to educate ourselves, and that's our responsibility. It's not the job of the members of a marginalized group to educate the group that holds power.

As for genderism and sexism, I'm baffled at people who lash out against gay marriage or transgender health care or who refuse to recognize the impact of gender inequities in everyday life. These are human rights issues, and there should be equity for all. In a perfect world, right? Alas, we're far from it. Said plainly, discrimination based on gender preference, sex assigned at birth, sexual preference, etc., has no place in our shared human lives—and that applies to Pagan culture as well as mainstream. If you see it happening, call it out and then do what you can to support the person or persons affected (and, if possible, to educate the others as indicated).

Plagiarism and Pirating

As a writer and college instructor, this one hits me where I live, and I think it's important enough to give it a forum on this page.

Plagiarism is defined as taking someone's work or intellectual property, using it for one's own purposes, and failing to give credit to the work's creator. In other words, the plagiarist pretends that someone else's work is their own.

Why is this a problem?

First, it's dishonest for someone to imply that they had an idea or completed a work when the content was actually completed by someone else. This is intellectual dishonesty and a type of theft in its most basic form. This is not okay.

Second, it's unethical and disrespectful to intentionally fail to credit someone for the work they did and the material they created.

Third, using someone else's work and presenting it as one's own is a shabby practice that doesn't result in learning. It's lazy. Research and write an article on your own and you'll learn from the experience. Copy someone else's work and you're not much better off than when you started.

It's simple enough to avoid plagiarism. Start by doing your own work. And then, if you find you must use source material created by others, *give them credit.* Do this via a direct acknowledgment within or attached to the material. For written work, handling sources requires two steps. First, enclose exact words in quotation marks and add a parenthetical citation; this should include the author's name at a minimum, e.g., (Smith), and may also include a date or page number, depending on the publication. Second, list the entire source in a bibliographic list at the end of the piece. Note that if you paraphrase or reword the material, you *still* must cite it as above, because even reworded, the ideas are still someone else's. For other materials, such as images, graphs, and so forth, get creative in terms of how you give credit, but absolutely make it happen and make it obvious. Adding a caption with source information is an easy way to do this. Don't worry too much about the format. Just do your best to give full, detailed credit to the person who owns the intellectual property.

I've heard people say, "Hey, if it's on the internet, it's free for the taking." To this I say *no*. Just because something exists on the web doesn't mean it's freely available! The internet is simply another medium for hosting and holding works, as is a magazine or newspaper or journal or easel or CD or...you get the idea. If the work belongs to someone else, you need to give them credit when using it, and you may need to get their permission to use it. This is true whether you use one sentence or several pages of their work. Remember that if you use someone else's intellectual property, regardless of shape or length, you *must* give them credit. Failure to do this is plagiarism, pure and simple.

If the work belongs to someone else, you need to give them credit when using it, and you may need to get their permission to use it. This is true whether you use one sentence or several pages of their work.

In another "Yay, internet!" moment, take some time to educate yourself on whatever issues apply, e.g., copyright law, creative commons, open educational resources, etc. This can take some digging. You might start with a simple google query. If you're close to a public or college library (Did you know that most college libraries are open to the public? Now you do!), ask a librarian.

Plagiarism can hit people in the pocketbook, too. People who write content, create art, make music, and so forth depend on the money from sales as a major source of income—maybe even the sole source. Every time someone makes a pirated book available as a free torrent PDF or makes a cheap version of a Tarot card set and sells it on Amazon or copies-and-pastes a painting or photograph instead of paying for a print, that artist-creator gets *nothing* for their work. When we download or buy these product-fakes, we become part of the problem.

We can avoid contributing to piracy problems by buying products only from reputable sources (direct from the author/artist/musician is always best) and avoiding torrent and online sites selling enormous catalogs of free PDF books for a few dollars. If money is a problem, using the local library or looking for inexpensive used copies of books are good solutions.

Environmental Responsibility

An important but simple way to end this essay is with a discussion about environmental responsibility. Climate change is real. The human population is exploding, and sources of food, water, and clean air are increasingly threatened, as are wild spaces. Every human on the planet should be taking this seriously. I've heard people say they're not sure their actions are doing any good when compared to the environmental damage caused by large corporations, the fossil fuel industry, etc. But I'll play the role of Pollyanna over here and say we need to do everything we can, even if our actions seem tiny in the grand scheme. It's our obligation as humans.

What can we do as Pagans to help protect the environment? Here are some simple things:

• Use candles made of organic waxes, like beeswax and vegetable waxes, rather than petroleum-based candles. Again, another option is to try making your own.

- Avoid using herbs whose numbers are being decimated, like white sage and palo santo. Find substitutes instead. Better yet, plant your own herb garden—this is also good for the planet and the bees.

- Keep fires small or find alternatives. Battery-powered lanterns and LED candles are two options. Wood fires release particles into the air that add to particle pollution (aka particulate matter) and reduce air quality.

- Buy stones and crystals from reputable providers. Be aware that many crystals today are mined unethically (often from child labor) and may be dyed and claimed to be something else. How do you know if a provider is reputable and if the stones are authentic? First of all, know enough about the stones or crystals to know what they should look like. You should be able to ask the owner how or where the materials were obtained. Second, you can always use the internet to research the store or shop you're using. Third, if you belong to a magical group, members may have had experiences with local shops and might be able to offer suggestions.

- Rely on tools and altar or practice materials made of wood, ceramic, paper, or metal, avoiding plastic (and especially single-use plastic) at all costs. This also applies to the cakes and ale celebrations that follow ritual.

- Have I mentioned making your own materials as much as you can?

These are simple suggestions, and they're only a start. The key is awareness: we only have one planet, after all. That's the truth, and we get to decide how to care for it.

Closing Thoughts

Everything in this and the previous part I essay boils down to a few ideas.

We humans are in this together, alone together, on this precious planet.

The Golden Rule of treating others as we would like to be treated has been expressed in a myriad of different ways throughout a myriad of cultures and traditions. The Golden Rule still holds true today and every day.

Practice kindness. Cultivate respect. Provide hospitality. Care for others.

Susan (Sue) Pesznecker *is a mother, grandmother, writer, nurse, and college English professor living in the beautiful green Pacific Northwest with her poodles. An initiated Druid and green magick devoteé, Sue loves reading, writing, cooking, travel, and anything having to do with the outdoors. Previous works include* Crafting Magick with Pen and Ink, The Magickal Retreat, *and* Yule: Recipes & Lore for the Winter Solstice. *Sue is a regular contributor to the Llewellyn annuals. Follow her on Instagram @SusanPesznecker.*

Illustration: Bri Hermanson

Magical Self-Care

NURTURE YOUR BODY, MIND & SPIRIT

Skeletons in the Cobwebs: Clear Away Your Inner Clutter

Melanie Marquis

As witches, we might spend a good amount of time practicing how to manipulate and utilize the forces of the natural world, but the most important realm we must learn to master is our own inner domain. A big part of mastering the self is to take charge of what's allowed to dwell within the spaces inside and outside the body that our soul may choose to occupy. When we have energies within us that are stuck and stagnant, hidden or suppressed, the natural flow of the spirit is hindered and we have limited access to our own power. If we don't process these things, our energies become locked in and rigid, and we're unable to create the space needed for better things to come in. Sometimes we hide such things from ourselves so well that it can take a long time to become aware of the underlying problem.

Discovering the things you try to hide from yourself jump-starts the process of reclaiming your inner space, your heart, your mind, and your magick. It's kind of like how you can clean out a closet by chipping away at it item by item, or you can take everything out, clean out the dust, and start fresh, putting back in the space only what you want to have in it. The second method is definitely more efficient, making it possible to get rid of unwanted stuff by the pile rather than by the piece. For the witch who seeks to maximize their power and remove all blocks to greater ability, such work is essential. Through my own experiences realizing things I had kept hidden from myself, I've made some discoveries that can help speed along and ease the process.

Discovering the things you try to hide from yourself jump-starts the process of reclaiming your inner space, your heart, your mind, and your magick.

Finding Answers in Our Shortcomings

A spell that fails is a bummer, but it can also be a clue to discovering inner blocks and obstacles you didn't know were there. Magick requires desire to fuel it and space for it to flourish, and when either is lacking, your spells won't work as expected. Sometimes spells don't work because we have something else within ourselves that is literally blocking the path of the magick in a way that is altering or limiting the results.

I experienced a clear example of this recently when I cast a spell to bring in more money. Over the course of the next week, I found several coins on the ground, including three pennies that were minted nearly a decade before I was born. I also got a very small raise at one of my side jobs. The magick had worked, just not nearly as well as I had hoped, or at least that's how I looked at it at first.

Then I realized that the spell had actually worked exactly as well as I had hoped, because I honestly wasn't very hopeful at the time that I had cast the spell. My sights were set low because my spirit was set low, dug in deep to an identity of impoverishment and a scarcity mindset that had trained me to keep my needs and desires to a minimum. I've largely overcome this mentality, but when I'm extra stressed or exceptionally down in the dumps, the little vestiges of these beliefs that I like to imagine are all gone begin to grow again, emerging from the shadows within the deepest, most hidden parts of myself.

I don't actually have a strong desire for money, even though I know it can make life smoother. Truthfully, I didn't need it or want it enough for my most recent money spell to be any more effective than it was. Looking deeper though, I was faced with a more unsettling revelation. The reason I don't feel a strong need or desire for a lot of money isn't because I'm so enlightened that I've rid myself of all forms of gross materialism; it's because I would rather convince myself that I don't have a need or a want in the first place than cope with my needs and wants going unsatisfied.

I thought I had processed through all that "tricking myself into thinking I don't need or deserve stuff" business when I was overcoming some disordered eating behaviors several years earlier. Yet here it was again where I didn't expect to find it, lurking behind a halfhearted bit of magick that yielded clear, yet less than stellar, results. Those old pennies my money spell manifested were messages from my ancestors, telling me to look to the past for insight. This scarcity

If there are any particular magickal goals that you find perpetually unachievable, look deeper into your desires and beliefs surrounding the topic. You might discover some beliefs that are limiting the potential for the magick to succeed.

mindset and survivalist coping mechanism isn't new to me; it's been carried on like a sacred tradition in large parts of my family line. It's difficult to entirely rid myself of the lingering effects of such beliefs. There are still little chunks of it here and there, standing in the way of achieving the things I tell myself I want but don't allow myself to actually desire. Magick needs true desire in order to operate.

An ineffective spellcasting attempt probably happens to every witch now and then, but when certain spells consistently fail to succeed as intended, it can point to a block in your own energies that you are not yet seeing. If there are any particular magickal goals that you find perpetually unachievable, look deeper into your desires and beliefs surrounding the topic. You might discover some beliefs that are limiting the potential for the magick to succeed.

Clues in the Clutter

Another way to unearth clues about things you're hiding from yourself is to look deeply at any physical blockages in your environment. Are there any areas of your home where you have personally accumulated an overflow of items? Examining the deepest layers of such places can reveal clues to blockages that could be preventing you from accessing your full power.

Let me offer an example. There's an area of my home that I refer to half-humorously, half-seriously as the "alcove of doom." It's kind of a short hallway that leads to nothing, a weird indent in the bizarre floor plan of my two-story duplex. It's neither a room nor a closet or a hall, but just a weird alcove that's become a makeshift storage area for everything ranging from arts and crafts supplies to Halloween costumes to random electronics.

When I finally got the courage recently to fully excavate this area, I discovered that most of the stuff filling the alcove fell into two categories: things that belong to other people in the household, which I therefore deemed to be out of my control, and stuff that I was planning to do at a later date, such as paintings to finish, craft projects to start, quilts to repair, and winter clothes to sort and store. Nothing remarkable, really, other than a remarkably huge mess. I found I own more pencils than I could ever use. I found three boxes of various cords that no one in the household could identify. What I found at the very core of all this mass of clutter, however, revealed a deeper problem that I hadn't previously realized.

At the very back of the alcove, nestled beneath a giant foam pumpkin head mask, was a bin full of stacks and stacks of precious photos of my children when they were babies, rolls and rolls of undeveloped film I never got around to developing, and the baby book I never finished filling in. This whole bin represented all the moments from my children's childhoods that I had failed to remember, failed to savor, failed to meet with my full heart and mind. In short, these forgotten photos represented to me all my shortcomings as a mother.

Overall, I'm a very good mother. I love my kids unconditionally and support them in who they want to be and what they want to do. But there is always room for improvement, and there are always regrets of things I could have done better. I hadn't kept up with all the chores. I hadn't done all the things I should have done or said

I would do. I hadn't developed all these rolls of film, or put those photos into albums, or filled out my second child's baby book. Deep down, there was this feeling of being absolutely terrible.

Once I acknowledged these feelings and looked at my perceptions objectively, however, I decided my failures in scrapbooking and film developing probably weren't enough to qualify me as the worst mom on earth. I had done my best, and I could do better now that I could let go of the guilt that had been taking up space in my spirit.

If you have any overfilled areas of your home, look closely at what comprises the clutter and what lurks at the deepest layers. If you find anything surprising, anything you greatly value or that evokes strong emotions, examine your intentions in placing those items there. Look for any signs of symbolism in the choice of objects surrounding or concealing the more significant or emotionally charged items. Such details can lead to discoveries of hidden blocks that could be limiting your emotional wellbeing as well as your magickal abilities. Anything within us that harms our confidence, that causes doubt, that causes us to hide away painful parts of ourselves, disallows our energies from flowing freely, thus limiting our full ability to cast effective magick or to be our full selves.

Ritual to Release Hidden Blocks

The purpose of this ritual is to help you discover and begin to dismantle any hidden blocks that could be holding you back. You'll need some small scraps of paper, a candle and something to light it with, and either a small cauldron or a fireproof bowl or dish. Place the candle securely in the center of the cauldron or other fireproof vessel, and light the wick. Notice how the wick, wax, and surrounding air are quickly transformed by the presence of the flame.

When you're ready, scan the energies and thoughts within you— all the memories, all the emotions, all that dwells within you that is not flesh, blood, or bone. Do you detect anything that doesn't belong or anything you find very unpleasant? Are there places within you that you would rather not examine too closely? When you find such a place, take one of the scraps of paper and rub it on yourself as if you're wiping away the stuff you would prefer to not look at in detail. You can rub the paper down each arm, across your chest, across your forehead—whatever feels right. Envision the paper soaking up some of the shadows and pulling them away.

Hold the paper scrap briefly in the candle flame to set it on fire, then drop it into the fireproof cauldron or dish. Repeat with more scraps of paper, one for each uncomfortable, shadowy place you sense within you. Then hold the candle in your hand and direct the flame to burn any remnants of the paper scraps until they're reduced to ashes. Rub some of these ashes on yourself, on your face, arms, or hands, then snuff out the candle. Take some deep breaths with long exhales.

Relight the candle in its holder.

Now imagine that you are literally peering within yourself with a bright light, perhaps envisioning the flame of the candle you have before you. Look behind the less comfortable places that you previously identified. What do you find? Is there a deeper level that perhaps reveals something that was hurt or lost? Do you find anything you care about that has been hidden and neglected? Do you find anything much worse than the more apparent shadows you found before? If so, speak these things back into the light, looking at the candle flame as you consciously decide to pull these parts of yourself up to the surface. Sit with these energies and let your mind be an objective observer. As the candle burns, direct any unwanted thoughts or negative energies into the flame to be incinerated and transformed. Allow any pleasant energies you find to stay with you. When you're finished, snuff out the candle.

The Witch's Craft

It is the witch's craft to master the art of working in harmony not only with nature but also with the self that is a part of nature. Self-discovery and self-improvement are just as much a part of a witch's work as is casting spells on a full moon. Discovering the shadows hiding behind the shadows, the skeletons in the cobwebs on the skeletons, is a great way to jump-start deep healing and magickal growth.

Melanie Marquis *is an award-winning author, the founder and producer of the Mystical Minds Convention, and a local coordinator for the Pagan Pride Project. She is the author of* Llewellyn's Little Book of Moon Spells, Carl Llewellyn Weschcke: Pioneer and Publisher of Body, Mind & Spirit (IPPY *Award Gold winner for Best Biography*), A Witch's World of Magick, The Witch's Bag of Tricks, Beltane, *and* Lughnasadh, *as well as the co-author of* Witchy Mama (*with Emily A. Francis*), *and the creator of the* Modern Spellcaster's Tarot (*illustrated by Scott Murphy*), *all from Llewellyn. She is also the creator of the independently published* Stuffed Animal Tarot (*with Aidan Harris*). *Melanie offers tarot readings, handwriting analysis, witchcraft services, and customized classes in tarot and magick. She is also a folk artist and crafter. Connect with her at injoyart@yahoo.com, https://www.melaniemarquis.com, facebook.com/MelanieMarquisauthor, or on Instagram @magickalmelaniemarquis.*

Illustrator: Tim Foley

Grief Work for Witches

Elizabeth Barrette

Loss and grief are nearly universal human experiences. The only people who avoid them are those who care about nobody and nothing, or those who die relatively young before they experience significant losses. We all face loss and grief, but we don't all feel exactly the same about them or deal with them in the same ways. Each person is unique, the circumstances of loss vary, and our culture influences how each of us experiences these things.

Some cultures do better at equipping people to cope with loss, while others tend to sweep it under a rug. Witches have an advantage because our religion grows out of nature, with its myriad cycles of waxing and waning, of birth and death and rebirth. This gives us ways of framing our grief as part of those cycles and taking comfort in the fact that nature wastes nothing, so nothing is truly lost; it only changes its form. Individual religions under the Pagan umbrella offer many variations on this theme.

Types of Grief

When talking about grief, people naturally think about death. It is the biggest and most permanent loss that most folks experience. However, it's not the only reason for mourning. We lose many things over our lives, some smaller and some larger. Each loss brings its own grief. This is not a bad thing, because the smaller ones give us a chance to practice our mourning skills before we get to the really big ones. Here are some examples of different types of losses.

Small losses:

• Losing an opportunity you poured your heart into

• Outgrowing or losing a favorite garment

• A close friend moving away

• Death of an acquaintance

Medium losses:

• No longer being able to do something you enjoyed

• Losing a major possession such as a favorite car

• Breakup of a significant relationship

- Death of a beloved pet or working livestock

- Death of a friend or neighbor

Large losses:

- Losing a career that's part of your self-image

- Major health crisis; loss of body part or ability

- Home burning down or otherwise destroyed

- Financial ruin and loss of security

- Moral injury or soul loss

- Death of a relative or close friend

Be aware of disenfranchised grief. This happens when the people around a mourner trivialize the loss, or the mourner feels like they can't talk about their loss for whatever reason. Disenfranchised grief adds insult to injury. It also increases the risk of more things going wrong, like complicated grief. It is important to respect the wounds of loss, both in ourselves and in others. Don't downplay a loss that grieves someone else, and don't let other people belittle yours either. Grief is completed only when we acknowledge it and work through it, so that it can subside into the overall pattern of life instead of stabbing at us continually.

Another thing to watch for is complicated grief. This happens when something disrupts the normal process of grief, causing the mourner to get stuck in it instead of progressing through it. You may have experienced a smaller "stuck problem" when something just kept nagging at you. These experiences offer good practice for getting unstuck by finding a way to sort through the issue so that it can be filed properly in your memory. Sometimes complicated grief can be worked through on your own, other times with friends, or you may look for expert help. One way or another, you need to jump-start the mourning process. Here are some risk factors for complicated grief:

- Low level of mourning skills

- Lack of support to make space for grief

- Unhelpful people making matters worse

- Crisis of faith that cuts off spiritual support

- Mental or physical issues that impair the ability to mourn

- Life-shattering loss, like losing home and job and family to a wildfire

- Multiple losses without enough time to process each one

- Loss that seems unnatural, like losing a child

- Complicated relationship with the departed

- Death that is sudden and shocking

- Death that is lengthy and messy

- Feeling like the loss was your fault

Grief Care

Grief care is support offered to people in mourning. It ranges from spiritual to psychological to practical. Clergy generally learn this as part of their training, since all religions have rites for the dead and most include some sort of pastoral counseling for the bereaved. Cultures vary in their traditions regarding how to help mourners beset by various losses, but most provide something—although in today's more mobile world, the community ties that used to support this aren't always as secure as they used to be. When available, grief care gives validation to the pain of loss, meaning to the human condition, and practical support to help lighten the load of responsibilities during the healing process.

At present, professional grief care is erratic in terms of availability and quality. There has been some great progress in terms of understanding how grief works, which better equips grief specialists to assist mourners. Most places now have support groups for various types of loss, and the Internet offers even more variety if you find online support helpful. Several excellent websites provide resources on many types of grief and coping skills. I've listed some of my favorites in the resources section at the end of this article.

However, there's an unfortunate trend toward pathologizing grief. It's a ubiquitous life experience and not a mental illness or personal failure. It's normal to feel terrible after a deep loss and to be minimally functional for days or even weeks. But for most folks, the clouds start to lift within a few months as they work through the mourning process. It's only a significant problem if a person can't cope at all or doesn't feel *any* better after several months to a year.

For Pagans who feel that outside support would be helpful, it can be difficult or impossible to find a Pagan-friendly caregiver, and that's really important when dealing with matters of death and grief. Some experiences common to witches are considered signs of mental illness by outsiders, like perceiving disembodied souls. Some practices

There's an unfortunate trend toward pathologizing grief. It's a ubiquitous life experience and not a mental illness or personal failure. It's normal to feel terrible after a deep loss and to be minimally functional for days or even weeks.

that are common in many cultures, like speaking with the dead, are disbelieved or condemned in others. A caregiver who doesn't believe in other lives may be poorly equipped to help a Pagan who does. This can lead to disenfranchised grief or mourning.

If a Pagan expert is unavailable, sometimes one may be found from a faith with overlaps. For example, a Buddhist or Hindu priest will probably understand about reincarnation. Interfaith chaplains are especially useful because they are trained to support any faith, and they're pretty common in places like hospitals and houses of worship that serve multiple congregations. Many Pagans look beyond local sources and find support online, where it's often easier to find other Pagans and do virtual rituals.

Anyone can learn the basics of grief care to support friends and family in times of loss. The most important steps are just to be there and to listen. Sometimes people need to talk about their feelings or reminisce; other times they just need quiet company. A fuzzy blanket or stuffed animal can offer contact comfort. Any kind of help with everyday tasks will free up the person's time and energy for grief work. Instead of asking if they need help, ask *how* you can help; it skips over the need to request help. Comfort food is not only soothing but also lifts the need to cook that meal. Tea and cocoa also help.

What Is Grief Work?

Loss causes emotional injury. Grief is the natural marker of a healthy relationship at its parting point. Grief work is the process of tending to that injury so that it heals cleanly instead of festering. When people ignore grief or don't know how to treat it properly, it's prone to causing more problems. That is sadly common in today's world.

Mourning is how we make peace with what we have lost, whether that means concluding a relationship or saying goodbye to something else. The pain and the grief work allow us to remember that this is now in the past, part of our life story, so we don't keep looking for it in the present. When the memories are filed properly, they are less likely to pop out at inconvenient times, but we can still take them out to savor on anniversaries or other special occasions.

Various frameworks describe how grief and mourning work. One model proposes seven stages: shock, denial, anger, bargaining, depression, acceptance, and hope. A longer set creates a kind of valley shape, going down and then coming back up: loss/hurt, shock, numbness, denial, emotional outbursts, anger, fear, searching, disorganization, panic, guilt, loneliness, isolation, depression, reentry troubles, new relationships, new strengths, new patterns, hope, affirmation, helping others, and loss adjustment. Not everyone may experience all of these stages, or necessarily in the same order; it's just a common example. The chaotic nature of grief that some people experience has been drawn as a scribble instead of a valley; this, too, is normal. However, if you find yourself in a given stage, you may be able to use that to search for resources that will help you in this part of your journey.

Some people experience what's called a dual process model of coping. In their everyday activities, they rock back and forth between loss-oriented experiences (intrusion of grief, breaking bonds, grief work, etc.) and restoration-oriented ones (life changes, distraction from grief, new roles, etc.). This works much like rocking your car out of a rut, which is a lot easier than trying to push it straight forward. Let it rock and eventually it will roll out. Grief work is like the pushing you do to move the car—and if it's really stuck, then you know to try adding more people or something to boost your traction.

Another perspective looks at the tasks of mourning. Common examples include acknowledging the loss, processing the pain, adjusting to life without what has been lost, finding new things or people to fill some of the gaps, and honoring the memory while moving forward. These processes of grief work make it possible to incorporate the loss as part of life without being permanently hampered by it. Most wounds heal in time, so look for ways to assist that.

The healthier a relationship you have with death, and the more supportive your community is, the more likely the experience is to be sad instead of life-shattering.

The healthier a relationship you have with death, and the more supportive your community is, the more likely the experience is to be sad instead of life-shattering.

Imagine standing at the edge of a forest with notable locations between one side and the other: a pond, a rocky hill, a flowered clearing, a burn scar, and so on. Different paths go through the forest, so you might pass all the landmarks in a common order, or only some of them, or you might thrash through the bush without ever finding a trail. It depends on how well you know where you're going and how to get there, and whether you expected the trip or fell into it unprepared.

Tools and Supplies for Grief Work

Grief work benefits from having appropriate tools and supplies. These tend to fall into three main categories: information, comfort, and recording. Preferably, stock things before you need them, as they're good for multiple purposes. Many of these also make good gifts to put in a care package after someone else suffers a loss.

Altar—Memorial altars, temporary or long-term, appear in many religions. An altar could be as simple as a picture of your loved one, a pentacle or other faith symbol, and a vase of flowers.

Blankets—Grief tends to leave people feeling cold and exposed. A blanket is like a warm hug you can wrap around yourself. Some modern sherpa or microfiber blankets are especially effective.

Books—Any book about loss and grief can help, but Pagan sources will be easier to use. A classic is *The Pagan Book of Living and Dying* by Starhawk, M. Macha NightMare, and the Reclaiming Collective. It's also helpful to have sources that are specific to where you live, as services and regulations vary; check local hospices, funeral homes, etc., as well as bookstores. Prayer books are useful, such as *The Big Book of Pagan Prayer and Ritual* by Ceisiwr Serith and *The Interfaith Prayer Book* compiled by Ted Brownstein.

Comfort food—This category includes warm soothing foods, light things that are easy to digest, fresh whole foods high in nutrition and life energy, relaxing or uplifting beverages such as tea, etc.

Craft supplies—Useful supplies include paper, stickers, embellishments, markers, adhesives, scissors, a sewing kit, yarn, ribbon, etc. These can offer something constructive to do, and they also work for capturing memories. You might make a memorial scrapbook or turn a loved one's favorite sweater into a huggable pillow.

Cuddly objects—Popular choices include pillows and stuffed animals. Hugging soft things provides tactile comfort.

Emotional first aid kit—This is a box of supplies for treating emotional injuries. Fill it with things for feeling better. Most of the other things listed in this section qualify, but keep a set in one place for easy use. It's also wise to include a list of contact information for people you can reach out to if you feel overwhelmed.

Fidgets—Keep a collection of small toys or curiosities that are quiet and interesting to manipulate. Stress balls, spaghetti bracelets, cloth marble mazes, twisty toys, stretchy hand exercisers, foot fidgets, etc., can help relieve restless feelings.

Fuzzy clothes—These work like blankets, only they're more portable. Clothes made of textured fabrics like cable knit or velour improve the tactile effects.

Music—Some instruments such as saxophones and bagpipes are generally associated with mourning because they have a "keening" sound. In the early phases of grief, gentle music like harp or flute provides comfort and reduces background noise. Later on, more energetic music like drums may help get things moving again.

Photographs and albums—It helps to remember what was lost, but people vary as to when they want to do this, immediately or later. Pictures and other mementos help keep the memories alive and provide talking points with other mourners.

Techniques for Processing Grief

A variety of methods help people process grief. This way, they can file it as part of their life story. Then it doesn't intrude so much as a distraction from everyday life. It is fairly easy to find detailed resources on these techniques, so you can build up a tool kit of them.

Cleansing—From smoke cleansing to a warm bath, these activities remove negative energy and make for a fresh start.

Contact comfort—Most people benefit from healthy touch when they feel upset. This can come from friends or family. Pets, especially purring cats, also help. Some people prefer a fuzzy blanket or pillow instead.

Emotional expression—Bottling up emotions is very risky, so people need ways to let them out. Crying or "primal scream" are helpful for some. Others prefer creative outlets such as writing, art, music, or dance. Feelings often don't translate well into words, so nonverbal methods may work better.

Grounding—Strong emotions can make the body feel distant, and grief often causes numbness. Grounding activities such as a body scan, a chakra meditation, or touching textured items can help to reconnect body, mind, and spirit.

Time-binding—This is what lets us remember those who have gone before and learn from them. Storytelling, reading and writing, photographs, timelines, and mementos are all examples of time-binding.

Rituals Around Death

All cultures have rituals around death. These vary greatly depending on how a given society or religion feels about death and the afterlife. Some focus on helping a dying person make the transition safely. Others concentrate on protecting the living from negative entities attracted by suffering. Most cultures include ways of remembering the departed, particularly on special occasions like a memorial holiday or the anniversary of their death.

Two examples of final instructions are particularly well-known. The Book of Going Forth by Day (or the Egyptian Book of the Dead) is a collection of funerary texts and spells to assist the soul's journey through the afterlife. Liberation Through Hearing During the Intermediate State (or the Tibetan Book of the Dead) is a collection of meditations and guides that span the approach of death and the soul's travel between death and the next rebirth. Less famous but very helpful for witches is *The Pagan Book of Living and Dying* by Starhawk, M. Macha NightMare, and the Reclaiming Collective, which includes rituals, prayers, blessings, and meditations for before, during, and after death.

Many holidays honor the dead. All Hallows' Eve has become Halloween, which explores not only death but also identity and social roles. *El Dia de los Muertos* (the Day of the Dead) has a strong family focus, including picnics in cemeteries. Pagans celebrate Samhain, when the veil between worlds is thin. They hold rituals and feasts to remember their beloved dead.

Some cultures and many individuals mark the anniversary of a death. They may gather with family, hold a feast of the deceased's favorite foods, or share pictures and stories. People often make a pilgrimage to the grave and clean the headstone or leave flowers and other offerings. This helps maintain relationships, even across the veil.

Conclusion

Like birth, death is a transition between worlds. These are natural, universal experiences. Everyone is born; everyone dies. Most people have children, and most people lose friends and family to death. These transitions are much easier to navigate safely if you understand them and have tools for coping with them. They don't have to be scary unknowns. They can be accommodated as the natural parts of life they are. This is why cultures and religions have supporting customs, tools and techniques, and rituals surrounding them. These things help us frame important life events as part of the larger human experience.

Resources for Grief and Coping Skills

My current favorite resource is the website *What's Your Grief?*
Check out the articles on grief on their blog.
https://whatsyourgrief.com
https://whatsyourgrief.com/blog

Speaking Grief focuses on how people deal with loss.
https://speakinggrief.org

Positive Psychology is awesome in general. Take a look at their entries on grief, which include ones for counselors and bereaved people.
https://positivepsychology.com/category/grief-bereavement

Farewelling offers resources on planning as well as mourning.
 https://www.myfarewelling.com
 https://www.myfarewelling.com/planning
 https://www.myfarewelling.com/planning/grief-and-loss

Bibliography

The Pagan Book of Living and Dying: Practical Rituals, Prayers, Blessings, and Meditations on Crossing Over by Starhawk, M. Macha NightMare, and the Reclaiming Collective. San Francisco: HarperOne, 1997.

The Interfaith Prayer Book: New Expanded Edition compiled by Ted Brownstein. Lake Worth, FL: Lake Worth Interfaith Network, 2014.

The Big Book of Pagan Prayer and Ritual by Ceisiwr Serith. Newburyport, MA: Weiser Books, 2020.

Elizabeth Barrette *has been involved with the Pagan community for more than thirty-three years. She served as the managing editor of* Pan-Gaia *for eight years and the dean of studies at the Grey School of Wizardry for four years. She has written columns on beginning and intermediate Pagan practice, Pagan culture, and Pagan leadership. Her book* Composing Magic: How to Create Magical Spells, Rituals, Blessings, Chants, and Prayers *explains how to combine writing and spirituality. She lives in central Illinois, where she has done much networking with Pagans in her area, such as coffeehouse meetings and open sabbats. Her other public activities include Pagan picnics and science fiction conventions. She enjoys magical crafts, historical religions, and gardening for wildlife. Her other writing fields include speculative fiction, gender studies, and social and environmental issues. Visit her blog* The Wordsmith's Forge *(https://ysabetwordsmith.dreamwidth.org) or website PenUltimate Productions (http://penultimateproductions.weebly.com). Her coven site, which includes extensive Pagan materials, is* Greenhaven: A Pagan Tradition *(http://greenhaventradition.weebly.com).*

Illustrator: M. Kathryn Thompson

Magical Self-Care
for Breakups

Deborah Castellano

What's more universal to a witch than a breakup? Whether your heart is broken or your ego is bruised, or even if it comes as a relief (my circle sisters say there's nothing better for one's skin than *joie de nouveau divorcée*), it's likely that your inner ant farm has been shaken up. While there is often a difference in scale and scope in breakups—breaking up with someone you went on two dates with is usually different from breaking up with someone you lived with for a long time, shared finances and chores with, and perhaps had kids with—the initial sting

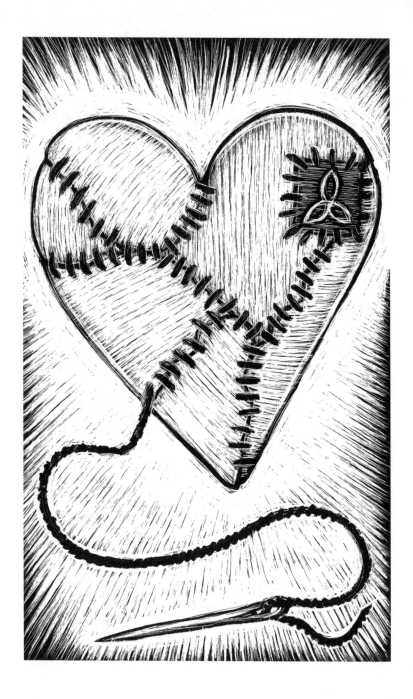

is usually pretty universal. It's the aftermath that is more of a spectrum, and that has more to do with if you were surprised or grateful for the parting of ways and how resilient you are, as well as how much your daily life will be changing as well. Then there are other factors like if you still have feelings for your ex, and how that affects your relationship with your kids (if you have them).

After a breakup, start by being gentle with yourself. You need a little (or a lot of) time to recalibrate your life. Don't make any big decisions that you don't absolutely, positively have to make until you feel recentered. If you're not sure how much time you need, there's nothing wrong with taking a week and going from there and reevaluating how you're doing.

How do you tend to act in a breakup? If you don't know, ask someone close to you. Do you get depressed or anxious? Do you tend to become more impulsive? Do you reach out to your support network for reinforcements? Do you give yourself time and space to feel your emotions, even the unpleasant or embarrassing feelings? Do you focus on something else, like going to the gym or crafting?

None of these feelings or coping mechanisms are bad unless they start negatively affecting your life. If you're not sure if they are affecting you in a negative way, ask a few people close to you and see what they think, and try to take in what they are saying.

Your healing process will be all about scale and scope, too. Eating ice cream for dinner for a night or two is no big deal. For a few weeks, it's a bigger deal to your physical health. No matter how big or small your breakup may be or how you cope generally with a breakup, you still need to eat and bathe, so you may as well add a dash of magic to it, along with some ritual work, to help you move forward.

It's okay to not be okay. It's okay to be overwhelmed. It's okay to be really excited. It's okay to feel happy again. No matter which way it's going for you (and that may be different depending on the day), you will get through this breakup one breath at a time.

Self-Clearing Ritual

This is a "cut and clear" spell, so it should be used only if you want to cut and clear all past negative emotions involving this person. There's always the possibility that you may clear that person out of your life entirely with this working, so be sure you are okay with that possibility. It may not be a wise spell to work if you have children together, as it could cause custody issues.

This ritual can be helpful to do when you are ready to move on so that you aren't bogged down by the past. You need one lemon, a knife, and sea salt. It is best to do this on a day when the moon is waning and is the smallest crescent. That said, you also need to be sure to block your ex from your socials and phone, or it's not going to be very effective. Intention is very important here.

Use the knife to cut the lemon in half. As you cut, using words or images, imagine being severed from your ex. Carve your name into one half of the lemon and carve your ex's name into the other half. Dip each open half of the lemon in salt to make the severing complete. Leave your lemon half by a crossroads by your home. Leave your ex's lemon half by a crossroads that is at least an hour away from you by whatever transit you use.

Self-Healing Bath Ritual

Healing a broken heart takes a lot of time and care, so a little magic to start the process can only help you on your healing journey. Let's start with a soothing magical bath to start mending the cracks in your heart, ideally on a Monday while the moon is waxing if possible. Put on your favorite breakup music, whether it's the "cry and feel sorry for yourself" variety or the "living well is the best revenge" kind. Light a lavender-scented candle and bring the flame close to your heart chakra, being careful not to burn yourself. Focus on healing your heart. Put some rose quartz crystals (for self-love) into the tub. Put some lavender-scented Epsom salt into the tub for healing. Get a nice face mask. Sheet masks are great for those who are less into glam, as you just drape the mask over your face. Get some cucumbers for your eyes. Pour yourself an apricot-flavored cocktail or mocktail so you remember to love yourself. Lie in the water and focus on being present with your feelings, whatever they are. When you've had enough, step out of the tub and put your hands in the water. Focus on putting all the negative vibes you have from your breakup into the water through your hands. Then pull the drain and watch the water flow away, envisioning any negative vibes about the relationship going down the drain with the water.

Self-Purification Shower Ritual (Scrub)

Even if your breakup was for the best or was initiated by you, doing a cleansing ritual will help you get a fresh start on the next chapter of your life. This ritual is ideally done on a Friday during a waning moon. Make a salt scrub with 1 cup sea salt (for cleansing), 10 drops rosemary essential oil (for releasing), 10 drops lemon essential oil (for clearing), 10 drops sage essential oil (for strength), and ¾ cup grapeseed oil. While mixing the ingredients together, focus on your intention to cleanse yourself from the breakup. Put the mixture in a sealable jar. Now add the same number of drops of these essential oils to a candle around the wick while focusing on feeling purified from your breakup. Run the flame of the candle from the top of your head to the soles of your feet, being careful not to burn yourself or light your clothes or hair on fire. You want to feel a little heat from the flame, but you don't want it to be so close to you that you get singed. When you get in the shower, use the scrub to remove anything you want to see go down the drain from your breakup so that you can move forward in your life.

Self-Care Smoothie

Chocolate heals a broken heart. Cherries and cinnamon bring future good fortune and happiness as you move forward in your life. Set your intention for what aspects of happiness, healing, and good fortune you want to give to yourself as you prepare and drink this smoothie so that it will be nourishing to both your body and your spirit. Blend the following ingredients with ice in a blender.

2 tablespoons cocoa powder

¼ cup frozen cherries

¼ cup quick oats

1 teaspoon mini chocolate chips

1 cup milk of your choice

½ teaspoon cinnamon

½ teaspoon vanilla extract

1 teaspoon honey

Self-Love Avocado Tartine

Preparing this tartine and eating it with purpose will support mending your wounded heart. Avocado works to replenish your natural glamour, and red pepper flakes work to speed up the healing process. Imbibe these ingredients with the intention to heal your broken heart quickly and to feel centered in your glamour again.

1 small avocado, mashed with sea salt

1 piece of pita

¼ teaspoon crushed red pepper flakes

1 hard-boiled egg, sliced (optional)

Put the mashed avocado on the pita and then the red pepper flakes and hard-boiled egg.

Self-Confident (Sex-Positive) *Puttanesca*

This easy recipe is a fun and exciting way to reclaim your sexual self, as *puttanesca* means "in the style of the prostitute." Use plenty of Venusian tomatoes so you'll have leftovers for when you don't feel like cooking.

7 anchovies, diced (optional)

1 can artichoke hearts, drained

1 can sliced olives (I like green), drained

1 carton mushrooms, sliced

1 small jar capers, drained

3 cloves garlic, diced

1 onion, diced

1 large jar crushed tomatoes

1 bay leaf

1 parmesan cheese rind

½ teaspoon crushed red pepper

Salt to taste

1 package bucatini pasta or fresh spaghetti pasta

Put everything in a large pot except the pasta. Let simmer on the stove on medium-low heat for an hour. Make the pasta according to the instructions on the package.

Self-Knowledge Nutella Banana Ice Cream

Who doesn't want to drown their sorrows in ice cream during a breakup? No human I know! This is a healthier version of ice cream made with frozen bananas to combat the breakup blues, along with plenty of Nutella. Hazelnuts bring us self-knowledge, which can only help when figuring out what you would like to do differently in future relationships while you are binge-watching your favorite show. You can hand-mash the bananas if you don't have a blender or food processer. The texture will be different, but it will still taste delicious.

3 frozen ripe bananas, sliced

1 teaspoon honey

½ teaspoon vanilla extract

¼ cup Nutella

Put all the ingredients in a blender or food processer and blend on high (or mix by hand) until there's an ice cream consistency. Freeze in a freezer-safe container for at least two hours before eating.

Deborah Castellano (New Jersey) *is the author of* Glamour Magic: The Witchcraft Revolution to Get What You Want (*Llewellyn, 2017*) *and* Magic for Troubled Times: Rituals, Recipes, and Real Talk for Witches (*Llewellyn, 2022*). *She is an independent maker of ritual perfume and other fineries. In 2006 she founded the first Steampunk convention, SalonCon. She enjoys old typewriters and record players, St. Germain, and reality television. Visit her at deborahcastellano.com.*

Illustrator: Bri Hermanson

Touchstones: Magic for When You Are on the Rocks

Dallas Jennifer Cobb

We all have difficult times. They are a part of life. Sometimes we are injured, our relationships change, or our employment shifts. Not only do we face personal difficulties, but these past few years have taught many of us how we are affected by larger societal issues. Whether it is a war raging just over there, the spread of a worldwide pandemic, living under the resultant lockdowns, or the barrage of bad news that we are bombarded with on a near-daily basis, we all can feel "on the rocks."

While this article offers magical ways to address and cope with difficulty, if you are in a life-threatening situation or are unsafe, at risk, or otherwise imperiled, please seek help through your local police, medical, or community crisis network.

This article was inspired by life during the pandemic and highlights ways I've found to ground, support, and resource myself so I feel more even-keeled despite my fear, despair, and anxiety. I've found ways to enable myself to get up and keep going each day, even when I feel like I am on the rocks.

I hope you find tools and tips within this article that do the same for you.

On the Rocks

Like so many people, I found the changes I faced during the pandemic to be frightening and destabilizing. Stripped of my routines and my regular workplace and ordered to stay at home, I felt totally out of sorts. There was nothing familiar to help me feel safe and secure, no routines to follow to get me through the day, no coffee breaks to bitch with friends.

Add on the strict orders to stay home. Isolated and living alone, I felt lost without my friends, acquaintances, neighbors, and community. I felt terrified of others and what they might infect me with. I couldn't go to the gym, the movies, or community gatherings. Suddenly it was just me.

As was the case with many people, my stress levels rose. My blood pressure shot up. Frequently I lay awake at night worrying, and when I slept, it was fitful and restless. Anxious and out of sorts, I ate too much comfort food and numbed my fear with binge-reading and Netflix overconsumption, escaping into fictional story lines that took me away from my rocky reality.

Rock Bottom

But my self-soothing ways were not serving me. One day, when I couldn't stop crying, I knew I needed help. The crying was compulsive, uncontrollable. I didn't really even know what it was about. I wailed and felt hopeless and helpless, desperate and alone. My mind raced, my heart hammered. I knew I needed to do something.

"Get up and get out of here!" my inner voice shrieked. So I did. Putting on my winter clothes, boots, hat, and mitts, I added a scarf over my mask and went out into the blowing snow. Not wanting to see any other people (danger), I walked to the deserted beach near my home.

And it was there that I found the small tools that saved me.

Tools to Save Yourself With

There are many lifesaving tools I could recommend, but for the sake of this short article, I want to focus on a powerful few. While I consider these tools "magic," they also have scientific recognition. The place where science and magic come together is a power space.

Neuroscience and trauma-based research document how the negative effects of trauma and stress can be neutralized and overcome by using three powerful tools: becoming grounded, finding supports, and resourcing ourselves.

BECOMING GROUNDED

In electrical terms, grounding is the technique used to move excess electricity (energy) back to the ground in the safest and most effective way, usually via a grounding wire. In physics, grounding removes a "charge" from an object by allowing the excess energy to transfer to another object. In earthing, we humans "ground" by connecting to the earth through bare feet. The resonant energy of the earth affects us, essentially slowing us down, grounding us.

In mental health practices, the University of New Hampshire Psychological and Counseling Services defines grounding as "a self-soothing skill to use when you are having a bad day or dealing with a lot of stress, overwhelming feelings, and/or intense anxiety. Grounding is a technique that helps keep you in the present and helps reorient you to the here-and-now and to reality."

When I arrived on the beach that day, I was fragile, jittery, and crying, lost in emotional torment. I realized the roaring waves spoke to the feeling inside of me. Like the raging water, I felt angry, tumultuous, and agitated.

I faced the gnarling lake with feet hip-distance apart. I felt the rage, movement, and power of the water, but I also felt something else. Below my feet I was aware of the solidity of the beach, the sand and stone, the earth. Dropping my attention, I began drawing the earth energy up and through me. I released my rage, fear, and grief and let the big, rough lake take it away. After a few long breaths of grounding and releasing, my chest stopped heaving.

In the days that followed, I walked to the beach every day. I planted my feet and began to cycle the low, slow vibration of the sand and rocks up and through me, and consciously released my excess energy. As I did this, I could feel the growing ease in my body, mind, emotions, and spirit. The more I grounded, the better I felt.

As winter gave way to spring, I removed boots, and soon I removed shoes altogether. Bare feet made grounding infinitely easier. In a few short moments I connected to the calming energy of the earth, and felt her hold me, ground me, and neutralize my anxiety.

FINDING SUPPORTS

Finding supports includes identifying people, places, practices, and things that help to calm and center you. In the solitude of lockdown, I began to scour the beach for things that made me feel better. Each day I looked for a "treasure." Sometimes it was beach glass, but usually it was a rock or fossil. Finding a treasure released within me a little surge of dopamine, the reward chemical, and I physically felt instantly better.

My Pagan training has taught me about the healing and spiritual powers of crystals. Picking up tumbled rocks from the beach, I was mostly aware of their solidity. I felt comforted by their unchangeable nature. Tucking a rock into my pocket felt supportive. The rocks gave me strength, comfort in quietude, and a sense of solidity. With my pockets weighted down, I felt less likely to "fly off" emotionally. I was weighty and significant.

Resourcing Ourselves

Resourcing ourselves is the process of consciously choosing to develop small practices and habits, rituals and routines that instill a sense of safety and calm within.

Having felt grounded, I learned more about grounding and added a wide variety of grounding practices to my repertoire. In need of feeling supported, I turned to rocks to provide stability and solidity to my life, and I began to research the wide variety of ways to use rocks magically. Learning more about rocks and their uses was a way to expand my ability to resource myself.

At home I began to place the rocks in special spots where I would see them and feel comforted. I might not be able to see my friends and feel supported by their smiles, but these rocks each brought a smile to my face. From their place in my home where I could see them daily, they became my "touchstones." Between Zoom meetings, and computer work, I could pick up and hold a rock in my hand and instantly feel calm and supported.

My grandfather always had a worry rock in his pocket when I was young. Sometimes he would let me hold this shiny black stone and rub my thumb in the soft groove that he had worn in it over the years. He told me, "I just put all my worries into this rock. It can hold it. And then I don't have to." So I found a smooth black stone that felt good in my hand and began to carry it around. Every day I slipped it into my pocket, and when I needed to feel soothed and relieved, I would slowly rub my thumb over the stone.

> **Rocks can be used as touchstones,…but they can also be used to reinforce magical intention. When you use a rock in a ritual, it becomes imbued with the energy of the ritual and can later be used to reconnect energetically.**

Rocks can be used as touchstones, as I did with my "worry" rock, but they can also be used to reinforce magical intention. When you use a rock in a ritual, it becomes imbued with the energy of the ritual and can later be used to reconnect energetically. Rocks can be used on an altar, representing north and the element of earth. They can also be used to solidify and anchor spells, and as charms that hold power and presence in ongoing magical conjuring.

Consciously choosing to use rocks provides infinite ways to resource ourselves in a multitude of magical, practical, and health-promoting ways.

Simple Rock Magic

Small white rocks have traditionally been known as spirit signs. If you are struggling with a decision or lack direction, look for a small, rounded, white rock. Often a smoothed piece of quartz can appear to glow when the sun shines upon it. It is a sign that you are on the right path and that spirit walks with you.

The spiral has long been held as a sacred symbol, symbolic of death and subsequent rebirth, sometimes depicted as Ouroboros, the serpent eating its own tail. Like walking the labyrinth, the fossil of a snail (gastropod or ammonite) can be used for spiritual seeking, its spiral also symbolic of the evolving soul. If you have fossils where you live, seek one. Otherwise, use a flat rock, and as you contemplate your problem, conundrum, or question, trace a spiral inward with your finger. When you reach the center of the rock, "let go" of your confusion. Breathe deeply and release. Now spiral your finger slowly outward, listening for divine guidance and inspiration.

Search for a hagstone, a rock with a natural hole through it. Looking through the hagstone enables witches to see into other realms and see beyond the ordinary. When you need another perspective or long to see things differently, look at your problems through your hagstone.

As spring warmed up that first crazy year, I began to find heart-shaped stones everywhere, some tiny and delicate, others large and heavy. A shaped stone felt like direct communication from spirit. Finding these stones helped me understand that the Goddess loved me and was always there, even when I couldn't be around other people. Subsequently, the heart shape became synonymous with community connections during the pandemic.

If you have a serious problem, go someplace where there are lots of rocks and begin to throw them as far as you can. With each toss, say out loud, "Go away, be gone, I release you, good riddance," and literally throw away your problems.

After working with energy, always shake any residual energy off your hands. When you feel clear of anything negative, gently rub your palms together, creating some heat and friction. Build a small charge of energy between your palms. Separate your hands and expand the energy, then consciously use this energy to create good.

Rock Solid

You can bathe your face in energy or fill your heart with it. You can surround your body in a protective energy shield or send good vibes to a neighbor as you drop off a heart-shaped rock on their front step. You may choose to gently trace the lines of a spiraling gastropod or throw your troubles away. Whatever you choose to do, know that rocks can be your healing allies. Whether as touchstones, charms, talismans, or pocket amulets, rocks can provide grounding and support, which enable you to better resource yourself. And this helps produce calm, ease, stability, and mental well-being.

Any time you feel "on the rocks," rocks can help you become rock solid.

Resources

University of New Hampshire Psychological and Counseling Services. "What Is Grounding." University of New Hampshire. Accessed October 2022. https://www.unh.edu/pacs/what-grounding.

Dallas Jennifer Cobb *lives in a magical village on Lake Ontario. A Pagan, mother, feminist, writer, and animal lover, she enjoys a sustainable lifestyle with a balance of time and money. Widely published, she writes about what she knows: brain injury, magick, herbs, astrology, healing, recovery, and vibrant sustainability. When she isn't communing with nature, she likes to correspond with like-minded beings. Reach her at jennifer.cobb@live.com.*

Illustrator: Tim Foley

Confessions of an ADHD Witch: Practicing Magick as a Neurodivergent

Monica Crosson

Once upon a time there was a Witch who lived deep in a forest in the Pacific Northwest, where tall trees and looming clouds protected the secrets of its inhabitants. In the cottage where she crafted her magick, she'd sometimes mutter to herself, for her mind never shut down. While doing mundane chores like sweeping the floor, she'd suddenly be inspired to create a spell and off she'd run to write down the words of enchantment before they dissipated into the cluttered corners of her brain.

When she finished jotting down the words of her spell, she'd place it in a drawer among the candles and charcoal tabs and bits of twig and bone and loose herbs she planned on organizing as soon as she found the time. But a quick glance through the warbled glass of her window would reveal a garden in desperate need of weeding, and her raucous brain would once again dictate that that was where she needed to be. So the sweeping, the spell, and the messy drawers would be quickly forgotten as she rushed to her garden to look for a hoe that she knew she had left…somewhere. Yes, this Witch's days were busy, but nothing ever seemed to get done.

The sweeping, the spell, and the messy drawers would be quickly forgotten as she rushed to her garden to look for a hoe that she knew she had left…somewhere. Yes, this Witch's days were busy, but nothing ever seemed to get done.

This Witch was also highly anxious in social settings. Conversational protocol was never her forte. Sometimes she found the energy in the room so unstable that she could barely speak. Other times she tried to fill the emptiness with conversation starters like "I had to give a potbellied pig an enema once" or "I have a totally cool way to banish that, but I'd need some of your urine." The mundane folks thought she might be crazy and her magickal friends thought of her as charmingly eccentric.

Early-morning meditations for this Witch were never successful, for her mind was constantly spinning. No matter what incense or music she chose, she'd twitch and tap as rapid thoughts infiltrated her zen. This upset her, as she didn't understand why she could never find the internal peace that so many of her peers described. What she did

know was that while she was walking through her enchanted wood, spinning, dancing near the river's edge, or talking to the trees, she was at her calmest, for movement in nature was her zen. As a writer, her first drafts were planned while she was in motion, either while rocking in an old wooden rocker that perfectly fit the curves of her body or while walking along familiar trails where her mind could drift freely.

She was also the one whom anyone could count on in her small community that sat within the enchanted forest, for she was clever and creative and, when pushed, could whip up a ritual, story, or party on demand. People knew this and came from far and wide for help. When focused on something she loved, she would spend hours combing through books and practicing whatever the craft might be until the fire that ignited her fizzled out—and her attention turned to another spark of light.

This Witch lived for years hating this paradox, for she was a procrastinator who could work efficiently when time demanded it of her. She was highly creative but felt she could never follow through with her creations. She required organization to thrive but could never get organized. She talked too little or too much. Her constructs were different from those around her: while her friends thought of finances and retirement plans and home and car insurance, she thought about new books on folklore, flavored coffee, and a new witchy subscription box. And self-doubt was her constant companion.

If you haven't guessed already, that Witch is me. And I'm sure there are many of you out there who can identify with my story. Far too late in life I was diagnosed with ADHD, or attention deficit hyperactivity disorder. As a child, I always connected this disorder to the disruptive boys in my classroom who smashed bugs in my books, but not to me. Not the shy girl in the corner who thought far too much about dragons and faeries and cared too little for math. But in hindsight I have to laugh, because it was me all along. I was the one with the wonderfully wacky brain who fought (and still does) to keep in line with a neurotypical standard of thinking. And I wish I had known then what I know now about my neurodiversity. Yes, those of us with ADHD think differently than others, and I've learned techniques to help me succeed in a neurotypical world. But I've also learned to appreciate the beauty and quirks of my not-so-typical mind.

Neurodiverse vs. Neurotypical

Neurodiverse individuals are those of us who think, behave, or learn differently from what is considered standard or typical. *Neurotypical* is the term used to describe those whose brain functions, behaviors, and processing would be classified as standard. The term *neurodiverse* originally focused on people on the autistic spectrum, but it has been expanded to include all people with variations of cognitive functioning. These include people with autistic spectrum disorder (ASD), ADHD, ADD, dyslexia, dyspraxia, dyscalculia, dysgraphia, Meares-Irlen Syndrome, hyperlexia, synesthesia, and Tourette Syndrome, as well as OCD, schizophrenia, dissociative identity disorder, bipolar, and other personality disorders. Neurodivergent people exhibit these conditions in many ways, and many of us have learned to mask our neurodivergent characteristics in order to fit in with the standards of a neurotypical world.

Neurodivergence and the Craft

For magickal practitioners who are neurodivergent, our magick may look slightly different from that of our neurotypical friends because our moment-to-moment experiences of the world and how we respond to them differ. It's important for us to remove any perceived limitations on how our magickal practice should look and instead design our practice around how our brain functions.

Meditation

Many of us who are neurodivergent feel and experience the world more intensely than a neurotypical person might. We are more apt to pick up on nuances of energy at play in a room, and we are typically the first ones to notice when something is off with an individual or situation. Light, sound, smell, touch, and taste all have an emotional effect on us, and we can become overstimulated easily. This makes meditation an important aspect of our practice. But because many of us (especially those of us with ADHD) have a hard time regulating focus, meditation can be a daunting experience. Mindful meditation may help. Here are a few variations to try:

- *Walking*: Make your next walk count. Instead of shuffling to your next location with only worries on your mind, use your time on foot as a meditative technique, with your eyes wide open and cognizant of your surroundings. Take in the rustle of leaves in the park or the crash of waves on the shore. Focus on the rhythm of your gait. Other forms of active meditation include jogging, swimming, spinning, and dancing. This is a great way to let go of the thinking mind and reconnect with our natural surroundings.

- *Cooking*: If you're a kitchen Witch, practicing mindfulness while preparing a meal is a great form of meditation. Take in the scents and focus on the ritual of grinding herbs and slicing vegetables.

- *Yoga, Tai Chi, Pilates, and other forms of gentle physical exercise*: These allow your mind to remain focused while practicing precise movements to enhance flexibility and strength.

Hyperfocus and Hyperfixation in Magick

Though those of us with ADHD and/or ASD may have a high degree of distractibility. Paradoxically, many of us experience both hyperfocus and hyperfixation, which can be a blessing and a curse. In extreme instances, we can forget to eat and sleep and can become neglectful of our surroundings. But for the most part, our ability to focus is a successful way for us to be productive and maintain engagement with a goal. This makes neurodivergents very powerful Witches.

Our ability to focus is a successful way for us to be productive and maintain engagement with a goal. This makes neurodivergents very powerful Witches.

Benefits of having a neurodivergent brain in spellcrafting include:

- A nearly inexhaustible amount of energy that can be focused on an intention

- A depth of focus that allows a neurodivergent practitioner to become an expert in any skill or type of magick they have an interest in, be it working with crystals or herbs, forms of divination, planning ritual, light work, shadow work, etc.

- The ability to get a lot done in a short amount of time—These are the Witches to go to when there is a ritual or spell that needs to be put together quickly and/or in an unconventional way. We have your back.

Go with the Flow

Creating magick that is conducive to a neurodivergent mindset is the most important factor of all. This means that how we put together a spell or ritual or organize our tools and supplies needs to flow with our thought process. Things to consider may include:

- *Use an easy organization system.* Notoriously unorganized, ADHD practitioners may want to keep magickal tools and supplies on open shelves for easy accessibility and to avoid cluttered drawers. Try drawing sigils on colored index cards or sticky notes that can be tacked onto a pinboard and pulled down as needed. Use marked plastic craft bead boxes to hold individual crystals. Paint canning jars for storing herbs or incense blends in colors that coordinate with their magickal intention.

- *Regulate focus.* When you're not in hyperfocus, include a worry stone or fidget tool while spellcrafting to help regulate your focus. Great stones for neurodivergents include green calcite, malachite, green aventurine, hematite, and tiger's-eye. These stones improve focus and can be calming.

- *Less is more.* Impulse spending can be an issue with some neurodivergents. Making your own tools is a way to save money and to utilize your hyperfocusing abilities. Found sticks can be made into wands. Large stones can be painted to symbolize deities. And buying beeswax sheets and rolling your own candles is cheaper than purchasing them.

- *Keep it simple.* Spells don't have to be elaborate. By keeping them simple, you can avoid becoming overwhelmed. Why use ten protective herbs in a spell when you can get by with just one? Keep altar setup simple, too, to avoid the temptation of leaving the clutter to be cleaned up later.

．．．．．．．．．．．．．

We neurodivergents strive for perfection. For many years I tried to keep up with neurotypical standards—and believe me, I cried many a tear because I didn't fit the mold. It was only when I was diagnosed with ADHD and embraced and accepted myself for the unique and powerful Witch I am that I really started to appreciate my gifts. If you've been struggling with ADHD symptoms, I urge you to see a doctor. Get a diagnosis and walk with your pointed hat high, for we do not fit the mold—and that is a blessing.

Resources

For more information on neurodiversity, check out these articles and websites on the Neurodiversity Network website: https://www.neurodiversitynetwork.net/articles-websites

Monica Crosson (*Concrete, WA*) *has been a practicing Witch and educator for over thirty years and is a member of Evergreen Coven. She is the author of* The Magickal Family *and* Wild Magical Soul *and is a regular contributor to the Llewellyn annuals as well as magazines such as* Enchanted Living *and* Witchology.

Illustrator: M. Kathryn Thompson

The Sober Pagan

Awyn Dawn

From enjoying cakes and ale during ritual to engaging in substance use to reach altered states of consciousness, it seems that psychotropic substances are often woven into the fabric of paganism. It is hard to find an event or gathering these days where there isn't at least a bit of weed in the vicinity. This freedom of choice is one of the parts of paganism that seems to attract so many. But what does this mean for the sober pagan? How can a person navigate this world and still keep their sobriety intact?

There are many reasons that a person may choose to engage in either long-term or short-term sobriety. These decisions are often personal, making talking about them not at the top of someone's to-do list. I don't think the reasons why a person gets sober need to be justified or explained to anyone. But having been put in situations in the past where I had to "defend" not drinking, I think it is worth opening the topic up for discussion.

Some people may abstain for health reasons, dietary reasons, pregnancy, because they are an alcoholic/addict, legal reasons, or sensitivities, and others may just not want to drink. All of these reasons are equally valid and should be respected as part of a person's sovereignty. It's not my goal in this article to teach you how to be sober; there are many programs in place for that already. It is my goal to help you learn how to fit sobriety into a pagan world.

If you are a sober pagan, one of the first things to understand is that others do not need to change their behavior for you. There will always be liquor stores, and any campout may have someone smoking pot by the fire. If you come to accept this as a fact, it will be a lot easier to accept when it happens and move past it. This being said, it makes me happy to see an increase in sober-friendly functionality in gatherings and event spaces. This includes things like nonalcoholic alternatives being passed around in circle, sober camping sections, and kid-friendly events that make it a bit easier to engage in public spiritual practices for sober pagans.

Asking Your Coven for Support

If the group you work with doesn't offer nonalcoholic alternatives, ask one of the officiants if these can be instituted. They might tell you no, but you are far more likely to get a yes, and you may even be asked to supply it at the next gathering. If you get a no, then perhaps it's time to evaluate if this is the right group for you. Neither answer means that the group has to stop passing the chalice of mead; it simply means that *you* get another option. When that chalice or horn comes around, you can still hold it up to the gods and goddesses, then move it close to your face but don't imbibe. If this is difficult for you, discuss with your high priest/ess the best way to incorporate the symbolism of ritual with your goal to maintain sobriety.

Solitary Practice

For those of you who practice solitary, it saves a whole lot of guesswork if you just opt for juice instead. I like to get those glass bottles of white, rose, or red grape juice (depending on the ritual intent). Not only are they inexpensive, but the glass bottle is recyclable and tends to have more of a ritual feel than the plastic versions. Do not worry that your juice will be "less appropriate" than an offering of alcohol. Never have I had an offering of such juice turned down. Never has my ritual been less powerful for using juice, almond milk, cider, or any other natural alternative.

Altered States of Consciousness

Okay, you've figured out how to attend ritual and stay sober. What about when you are ready for the deeper magicks, specifically trance work and altered states of consciousness? When I was a neophyte, I didn't know much about trance states. I thought that a person had to use a lot of drugs to reach an altered state of consciousness. There are a couple of things very wrong with this idea, which I am glad to clarify. The first is that those who use substances in a spiritual manner to achieve a trance state don't use them to the point of excess. They know the exact amount they need. They also respect the substance. It is not about getting drunk or high for them; it is about tuning in to the other realms to do the work they need to do.

Luckily a person can enter a trance state without using any substances at all. Some of the methods used historically included drumming, dancing, and repetitive action (such as spinning wool, sewing, and weaving). Until recently, the women of villages would get together and spin and weave, not only to fulfill an important societal function but also to open themselves up to messages and insights by entering a trancelike state. Sitting at a crossroads, especially in the moonlight, and performing one of these tasks is a powerful way to connect to Hekate. If you live in the city, you may elect to use a doorway between rooms as a crossroads without losing any of the intention.

Luckily a person can enter a trance state without using any substances at all. Some of the methods used historically included drumming, dancing, and repetitive action (such as spinning wool, sewing, and weaving).

There are other ways besides the use of substances to induce a trace state, some intentional, some not. You may have experienced driving on a stretch of road and suddenly miles have passed but you don't remember the drive at all. That was because you entered a trance state, albeit unintentionally. To create an altered state for ritual purposes, you can create art, chant malas, recite a *vardlokkur*, drum, clap, spin wool, weave, sing, and dance, just to name a few.

How the Community Can Help

For those of you who have not had much interaction with sober pagans, one of the main steps you can take is to avoid asking why someone is electing not to drink. It's natural to be curious, but it's nobody's business. It's also rude to ask someone this question, as the answers are sometimes painful. So when someone says they are sober, just say "okay, welcome!" and let them know where their alternative ritual drink is.

When hosting a public gathering, try to provide a nonalcoholic alternative. It should be clearly labeled, accessible, and available to anyone who wants it without having to ask. For rituals, a few sentences can be stated by a designated group member regarding which cup contains alcohol and which doesn't. It doesn't have to be complicated.

For the Sober Pagan

Being sober is not something to be embarrassed about ever. It is a mark of pride, and it is okay to talk about it, discuss it, and advocate for your sobriety. This is harder for some to do than it is for others. But look, we don't live in 900 BCE. We live now. In our modern world, alcoholism, addiction, STDs, and a greater instinct for social justice and personal autonomy exist and deserve to be acknowledged. You don't have to talk about your reasons for getting, being, or staying sober. Just know that if you choose to, you are not alone. There are more sober pagans than you might think.

Blessings.

Awyn Dawn *is the author of the award-winning book* Paganism for Prisoners: Connecting to the Magic Within *as well as* Paganism on Parole: Connecting to the Magic All Around. *She has appeared as a guest on many podcasts and radio shows and has written for* Spirituality & Health *magazine. Over a decade ago, she found herself incarcerated. Using Wicca and other pagan spiritual paths, she overcame the cycle of recidivism. She now devotes much of her time to writing books encouraging spiritual growth and development for those in and out of prison. She is currently earning her MFA in creative writing in London.*

Illustrator: Bri Hermanson

Witchy Living

DAY-BY-DAY WITCHCRAFT

Finding Your Voice: Exercises to Activate and Balance Your Throat Chakra

Michelle Skye

Outside, in the gray light of dawn, a lone rooster stands in the grass. He looks around, pecks at the green bits at his feet (maybe hoping for a worm), and crows with abandon. Then he does it again, and again, and again. Even after the sun comes up, his voice echoes around the farm as he practices adding his voice to the volume of the world.

I think it's no coincidence that in the world of poultry, the rooster is the most well-known for his noise. His voice reflects his prowess and strength, drawing hens toward him to perpetuate the species. The hens make sounds too, although not many people notice this.

When they are content, amid the flock, they hum deep in the back of their throats, creating a soft song that threads and winds among the whole flock. When the hens are struggling (which sometimes happens when they lay an egg), they screech and make a loud cackling sound that alerts the farmer to their distress. When the hens are scared, they flap their wings loudly and make sharp staccato calls that bounce from one hen to another as they form a natural alarm system.

I know this because I live on a chicken farm. (I have for a lot of my life!) For me, the example of the hens and the rooster illustrates an important truth: sometimes it's hard to get your voice out into the world because someone else's song drowns you out. Just as the hens on a farm are overshadowed by the rooster, the noise of someone else draws others' attention away from you. Maybe this has happened so often that you have stopped trying to express yourself in the world. Your voice quiets. People have a hard time hearing you, even if you are the only one talking. And the voice that the Goddess gave you disappears.

You just need to exercise the muscle of your voice to activate its power. Like any muscle, the voice needs practice, and if you've been holding your voice back for years, it can take time to reach your full strength.

But not really. It's still there, hiding behind the years of being silenced (by others, by society, or by yourself). You just need to exercise the muscle of your voice to activate its power. Like any muscle, the voice needs practice, and if you've been holding your voice back for years, it can take time to reach your full strength. Even a rooster has to practice before he makes those distinctive cock-a-doodle-doos.

So go ahead and try some of the exercises in this article! Practice them by yourself and discover the pleasure of hearing your own voice out loud, laughing and expressing joy! Then share that joy with others. Your voice has value. Your ideas are unique because they are yours. With these exercises you will begin to realize that your words have merit and will benefit other people if you just choose to share them.

Judgment-Free Zone

Opening up your voice, after it has been shut down, can feel daunting. I have been on a journey of opening my voice for a lot of my adult life. At some point in my early childhood, I learned that keeping quiet was better than speaking up. I cannot pinpoint when this inner belief took root, but by the age of twelve I was well on my way to being the "quiet one" at school.

In seventh-grade French class, I never raised my hand, even if I knew the answer. When my teacher threatened to no longer call on me because I refused to raise my hand to answer questions, I breathed a sigh of relief. No more being forced to talk in class. Of course that only lasted a week or two until the teacher realized I was stubbornly throwing my grade away. In chorus that same year, I sang proudly with the group, confident that any mistakes I made would be covered up by the other singers. This illusion was shattered when a girl in front of me turned around one day and said to me, "Wow! You really can't sing, can you?" After that, I sang much more softly.

In both of these instances, my voice was being judged by others. In French class, the teacher constructively criticized my word choice, sentence structure, and accent in front of the class. (It was her job after all.) In chorus, the student in front of me rudely commented on my singing ability in front of other classmates. Our inner critic takes these experiences and, because they feel uncomfortable in the moment, makes the decision to avoid anything that is similar in the future. (Does this sound familiar?)

After seventh grade, I did my "speaking" in writing form until I became a mother. My child was a wiggly, excitable toddler who did not like going to bed (like most toddlers!). In order to calm her down before bedtime, I would turn out the lights and have her lie down in bed and listen to a story that I made up on the spot. This story was not written down or planned and practiced ahead of time. Instead, it spontaneously flowed from the moment that unfolded between my child and me. This was my first foray into judgment-free vocal expression. My child would stare raptly at me as I spun the tale for her. She never complained or criticized. She did not point out flaws. She simply enjoyed the quiet moment between us.

Using your voice pushes you out into the world. By revealing yourself, you become vulnerable and open to the possibility of other people's negativity. To begin your journey in exercising your voice, start in a judgment-free zone. Perhaps you schedule time at the local pound and read to the animals. (Reading to a dog is super helpful for kids when they are first learning, as the dogs just enjoy the experience without commenting on any mistakes.) You might reach out to an elderly facility near you to visit folks who are lonely and looking for conversation. Volunteering at a local preschool or elementary school can also help you gain confidence in your voice. Another, more radical idea would be to enroll in an acting class. The voice is the tool of the actor, so a beginning course would teach you exercises for using your voice.

All the World's a Stage

Have you ever watched *High School Musical* and tried the vocal exercises that Sharpay does right before she goes on stage? She purses her lips and vibrates them as she makes a high-pitched sound in the back of her throat while she waves her hands in front of her face. It is hysterical and ridiculous! It makes you laugh, both when you see it and when you do it. For this reason, it is an amazing icebreaker for anyone who is opening up their voice for the very first time. I recommend trying it by yourself in your bedroom or living room. Once you have become comfortable with the exercise, practice it in the mirror. Connect to yourself as you make these crazy sounds, and know that it's okay to be silly!

Tongue twisters are another fabulous way to laugh while using your voice, mostly because they are also completely absurd and outlandish! Actors use these tools to warm up the mouth and the vocal cords so they will be more flexible on stage. By doing these silly exercises, actors learn to be comfortable with their vulnerability (a key component of vocal expression), and their words will be crisp and clear. You probably remember some tongue twisters from your childhood, but here are a few with which to practice:

She sells seashells by the seashore.

Peter Piper picked a peck of pickled peppers.

Which witch is which?

Gobbling gargoyles gobbled gobbling goblins.

I dare you to say these out loud without laughing! They are so silly. It's even more fun when, with each repetition, you speak faster and faster and faster! It's harder than it looks, but that's the point. The tongue twisters are ludicrous, but the laughter that ultimately ensues helps to shake up any old beliefs that may be holding you back from expressing yourself. Laughter is a wonderful tool for breaking up stuck energy. As you get more and more comfortable with speaking these tongue twisters into the universe, using your voice to evoke fun, challenge your friends and family members to a Tongue Twister

Talk-Off. See who can say the fastest tongue twisters without messing up! Bonus points if the volume is so loud that the neighbors start wondering what kind of fun you're having. (Don't be surprised if they ask to join in!)

Affirmations and Incantations

Tongue twisters are, of course, the precursors to affirmations and incantations, the very foundations of voice magic. Affirmations help us to shift unhealthy beliefs and patterns in our own minds and bodies. Incantations are spells that allow us to manifest change in the world. One works internally and the other externally. Both are powerful tools for bringing one's voice into the world.

I recommend starting with affirmations, as they will give you the space to explore your inner beliefs and shift any that are holding you back from using your voice. An affirmation is a statement that you create and state out loud that expresses a positive belief. Affirmations are positive in nature and focus exclusively on the self. They can shift the way you see the world. They help heal emotional, mental, and physical traumas and wounds. Although they are not a replacement for medical attention, affirmations can supplement regular medical care by supporting change and well-being.

Affirmations do not have to be spoken in a particular format or style except as statements of fact rather than requests for possibility. In other words, you state the truth as you wish it to be. Affirmations can be simple or complex, depending on the person who creates them. However, they are usually stated aloud, which is why they are so fabulous for opening up the voice. A good time to say your affirmations is in the morning, right after brushing your teeth. This sets a positive tone for the day and reminds you of your own self-worth before venturing out into the world. Try stating your affirmations while gazing into your own eyes in the mirror for a truly transformative experience! Remember to state the affirmations in a repetitive format, as that helps to cement them into the subconscious brain. I recommend picking a magical number that calls to you and using that as the repeating pattern. Here are some examples of voice-specific affirmations that I have used over the years:

I am safe to use my voice. The universe supports me.

My unique voice has power and merit.

My voice is beautiful and people long to hear it.

Incantations are slightly more complex than affirmations because they are spellwork designed to manifest change in the world. They have been utilized to create health, remove pests, attract love, and curse enemies for over a thousand years, with some of the oldest incantations being found in ancient Mesopotamia and ancient Egypt. Incantations are not always focused on the positive, but they are usually focused on transformation. Incantations work to effect a shift in the world. While this may include the magic practitioner, this form of word magic can expand to include all aspects of life on this planet.

Modern incantations tend to lean toward a flowery, poetic format. Many practitioners find it helpful to use older speech patterns and phrases. They rely on rhythm, rhyme, and syllable count to separate the spell from everyday speech. Get out your high school English textbook because all those notes on Shakespearean sonnets are going to come in handy! Common verse types in incantation spells (as well as Shakespearean sonnets) include quatrains (four lines) and couplets (two lines). However, an incantation can technically be as long or as short as the spellworker wishes, as long as the verses and words state the purpose of the spell. This is the key to incantation magic. Your words have power. The words you use will shift your reality. Here are a few incantations that are common in magical practice, along with a brief explanation of the poetic devices used in each:

- As I *will it*/*So mote it be*—This is a non-rhyming couplet that employs four syllables per line, along with an archaic sentence structure and word choice.

- *Stay if you will*/*Go if you must*—This is another non-rhyming couplet with four syllables per line, but it adds repetition of sentence structure to bind the two phrases together.

- I *open my voice*/*By will and by choice*—This couplet has five syllables per line and includes a rhyming component to add a pleasing singsong quality that makes the phrase easier to remember.

- *My chakra clears*/*My voice awakes*/*I free my fears*/*First step, I take*—Here is a quatrain utilizing four syllables per line and a traditional ABAB rhyming format (where the first and third lines rhyme and the second and fourth lines rhyme).

Vishuddha Chakra, Activate!

The Vishuddha chakra is the fifth chakra and is located at the throat. The chakras are energy centers that help us to stay aligned in our bodies. There are seven major energy centers that start at the base of our spine and go up to the crown of our head. When one (or more) are energetically off-balance, it causes a disturbance in the way energy flows through the body. It becomes more difficult for the energy to move easily when blockages are in place at any of the seven chakra points. If you have been stifling your voice, it is likely that your fifth chakra is not as energetically attuned as you want it to be. Here are some ideas to jump-start your throat chakra.

1. **Wear blue.** Sky blue, powder blue, turquoise blue, royal blue…really any shade of blue will resonate with the fifth chakra. When you choose your blue outfit for the day, state your intention to activate and heal your throat chakra.

2. **Eat blue foods.** Blueberries, bluefish, and blueberry bread, muffins, or donuts are great places to start. I actually crafted an entire week of blue years ago, which included eating only blue food. I had to be super creative! One of my favorite dishes was Alfredo macaroni and cheese that I dyed with blue food coloring. It was turquoise and so much fun to eat!

3. **Carry or wear blue stones and crystals**. Don't be surprised if the stone feels uncomfortable to you at the beginning of your voice-opening process. Sometimes a chakra has been shut down for so long that the energy of the crystal feels like it's putting pressure on the energy center. If this happens to you, slowly acclimate the crystal into your auric field by holding it for short bursts of time. As you become more and more connected to the crystal's energy, you can extend the time until you're wearing or carrying it for an entire day. Here are some of my favorite fifth-chakra crystals:

• *Blue lace agate:* A beautiful light blue stone with white striations, blue lace agate exudes a gentle calming energy. As it is an agate, it also has a substantial, grounded feeling, so it will help you bring your voice forward onto this earth plane.

- *Larimar:* A turquoise-colored stone associated with Lemuria and the sea, larimar will help heal any trauma you experienced when using your voice in the past, while activating your fifth chakra. It is also a wonderful stone to use to connect the throat chakra to the heart chakra.

- *Angelite:* With a creamy, soft blue color, this stone connects to angel energy, making you feel protected and secure as you venture into opening your throat chakra. Its energy signature is very calming and nurturing, yet it is a powerful ally in opening up the fifth chakra.

- *Aquamarine:* A translucent light blue stone that is the birthstone of all those born in March, aquamarine brings sea and air together to activate the fifth chakra. As it is a stone for creativity as well, aquamarine would be a wonderful choice if you want to bring your voice into the world through song, drama, or vlog.

4. **Chant the bija mantra *Ham*.** A *bija mantra* is a one-syllable seed sound, and Ham is the sound associated with the Vishuddha chakra. You chant it as you would Om, which, incidentally, is the seed sound of the third eye (Ajna) chakra. I recommend chanting Ham repeatedly for at least five minutes. (The way to pronounce Ham is "h-ah-m." The vowel sound is the same as that found in dog or log.)

. . . .

Through vulnerability, laughter, color, food, crystals, and (most importantly) the spoken word, you can open your voice and share your ideas with the world! It may seem scary at first, but you can start by remembering that your voice is a unique Goddess-given gift. By exploring and overcoming your old patterns of behavior, you can rewrite your inner ideas about the power of your voice and balance your Vishuddha chakra for your mental, emotional, and physical health. Try just one of these exercises and before you know it, your voice will be heard by many and will be a powerful force in the world!

Michelle Skye *is a dedicated tree-hugging, magic-wielding, goddess-loving Pagan. While she is best known for her three goddess books,* Goddess Alive!, Goddess Afoot!, *and* Goddess Aloud!, *she also works closely with many gods and male magic practitioners. Michelle is fond of reading (a lot!), rainbows, crows, oracle decks, walks in the woods, Middle Eastern dance, spellwork, grunge music, silver jewelry (especially if it's sparkly), and quirky '80s movies. She creates crafts and spells with her magic circle, the Crafty Witches, and celebrates the sabbats with her family coven at home. She has been spinning magic into the world her whole life but has been following the Pagan path for just over twenty years.*

Illustrator: M. Kathryn Thompson

Beauty and the Beat:
Take a Daily Beauty Break

Alise Marie

As a creature who has always forged an artistic path, I have often found myself unceremoniously plunked down in the midst of that all-too-familiar paradox where creative freedom collides with the necessity of the "day job." In the acting world, it is referred to as the "survival job," and I've heard life coach types more kindly call it the "bridge job," though I'm not sure it's a bridge to anything other than your bank account. Whatever its guise, a day job seems to be a given when you've chosen a creative life, particularly of late. I do recall—and I promise this is *not* through a rose-tinted lens—days of

old when one could reasonably get by on a fairly pleasurable blend of gig income and something akin to a café or shop placement, though now they seem like very distant memories. In this ever-expanding world of subscriptions, shortages, and skyward rents, one simply must find a way to do it all.

The Birth of the Beat

And so, several years ago, I found myself in *the* most horrendous (but, thankfully, part-time) position, wherein I would regularly inform my friend and similarly distressed coworker, "I'm going in the bathroom to hide." She would nod knowingly, and with a rather stoic facial expression, as she silently agreed to keep my covert flight a secret. Yes, these escapes always felt *slightly* overly dramatic—whisking away, flinging the door closed, bolting it with fervent passion, and heaving myself upon the vanity with a forceful sigh—yet they were also entirely necessary and, to me, quite the reasonable thing to do. I was able to *breathe*—enough, at least, to straighten my spine and get back out there.

And yet I knew there had to be a more empowered way to approach this level of stress I was experiencing. The possibility of a saucy final exit with a few well-chosen insults to the management, though relished, wasn't really in the cards, nor would it have been my smartest move ever. But clearly something had to be done. Little did I know that the simplest, most effective *petite ritual* was about to show her gorgeous self to me.

As they always do, the goddesses of beauty and love came to the rescue, and guided me in a practice of recharging myself with their unique magick: by taking a sacred pause, whenever needed, to reconnect with my body *and* spirit. I had always known the way back to my own power was through reconnecting with my body, feeling the sensations that emotions or thoughts had triggered, and relaxing into the senses. What I *hadn't* realized was that I could incorporate these pauses into my workday. Instead of a highly theatrical huff and a door slam, I would calmly, and with authority, simply excuse myself to the powder room, as anyone would. Armed with a few highly potent consorts and a certainty that this was my space to claim, I would perform a little ceremony that I like to call the Beauty Break. And it is exactly that: a moment to reclaim your divine feminine power.

Think of the Beauty Break as a reset button.... It's like those sacred pauses during meditation where thoughts are quieted and breath is all that matters.

Think of the Beauty Break as a reset button, or, more poetically, as the beat between the notes in music where the absence of sound actually allows your ear a moment to receive more rhythmic information. Remind you of anything? *Mm-hmm.* It's like those sacred pauses during meditation where thoughts are quieted and breath is all that matters. And the true beauty of it is that you can take a Beauty Break whenever the need arises, and it requires only two things: holding your own space and a well-edited bag of tricks.

Tools of the Trade

Let's talk about the bag you'll use for your Beauty Break. That's the fun part. Unquestionably, it must be absolutely *gorgeous*—perhaps velvet, brocade, or embroidered satin to start, but anything that makes you feel like glamour on fire will do. I love to discover vintage evening purses that, sadly, are far too tiny to conceal a cell phone and therefore must find a new purpose. Browsing local artisan boutiques, bazaars, charity shops, and online treasure troves like Etsy are a fabulous way to support budding talent and give fresh, eco-chic life to old finds.

Look for exquisite linings to offset the contents and give you something silky to brush your fingers against when you reach for them.

And what of these mysterious contents? Ahh...*that* is where the magick lies. I refer to it as my Mojo Bag, because really, that's what it is. Inside dwells the glorious potions to completely *transform* you from an overloaded emotional ragamuffin to a confident, powerful force to be reckoned with. Miniature vessels filled with a beautifying skin mist and serum combo, a talisman or amulet, a small vial of perfume, a crystal or two, and, of course, a killer lipstick will do the trick. (In amongst the baubles, I always carry a bit of my cat's shed fur straight from the brush for feline power and protection.)

Holding your own space…can be a challenge. We have become conditioned to deny ourselves what we *need* to thrive, and that can be as simple as taking time to sit down to a meal, getting enough rest, and consciously seizing the moment when we must revitalize ourselves.

Of course, holding your own space, and often even committing to claim it in the first place, can be a challenge. We have become conditioned to deny ourselves what we *need* to thrive, and that can be as simple as taking time to sit down to a meal, getting enough rest, and consciously seizing the moment when we must revitalize ourselves. I have had clients tell me the single most difficult thing to embrace on their wellness journey was to just claim that time and space for themselves. Taking care of our wellbeing should *never* be something we omit or apologize for. I find, too, that the Beauty Break is an easy way for even the most unassertive person to get what is needed—after all, *everyone* goes to the powder room.

Shapeshifting into Beauty

Once you've excused yourself (or, better yet, made a firm *statement* that you will be back in a moment), grab your Mojo Bag and make a beeline for the restroom. From the minute you make the decision to reclaim yourself, it's important to adjust your carriage. Walk as coolly, slowly, and confidently as you can—no harried scrambling or apologetic hunching will do: Goddess power has intervened. Now close the door and lock it if that is an option, because this white-tiled cupboard of functionality has just officially become a temple.

Stand in front of the mirror, place your Mojo Bag on the counter, and close your eyes. Take three long, deep breaths. Breathe in slowly through your nose, then gently exhale through your mouth. The first breath cycle will feel slightly tight, but by the third you should be purring along in a peaceful, deliberate rhythm. Be sure to stand straight, head held with purpose, shoulders back slightly and down. Now open your eyes. Who do you see in the mirror? Someone who's simply *had* it? Look deeper. The eyes are windows to the spirit, and right now you must seek to locate that spirit, and connect to it. See that flicker? That's your inner fire—*your life force.*

Stare deeply, fixedly, into your own eyes in the reflection. As you continue to breathe, focus on the flame returning to your eyes. Connect with that internal power, and say silently (or whisper, if you are out of earshot) something that resonates with you, a simple chant or mantra that brings you back to your own presence and strength. Keep it confident, be firm, and steer clear of blaming others or making comparisons.

Slowly wash your hands, but don't rush! Do it sensually. Pat them dry with care—after all, they do *so* much for you. Now reach into your Mojo Bag and take out your facial mist. Throw your head back and give your face and neck a fabulous spritz. Next, drop a bit of serum onto your ring finger, warming the potion by lightly massaging it with the opposite ring finger. Now gently dab around your eyes, in the smile lines, at the forehead expression points, and on your cheeks, pressing in ever so slightly. Rub your temples softly, caress your earlobes, then cross your arms and slide your fingers down the back of your neck, massaging as you go, all the way into those perpetually tensed muscles on either side of your vertebrae, arriving at your shoulders. Give them a good squeeze, and remember to keep breathing. With one last tiny drop of serum, massage around your mouth and into your lips. (This feels *incredible* and it softens all the tension you've held in your mouth, bringing fresh blood to the surface to create a plumper-looking lip.) Feel yourself relaxing into this delicious state. Your face will already be transformed by all this love, but we'll do a little touch-up to polish the apple, for extra potency: Dab a bit of concealer, brush your brows, refresh your eyeliner if it's headed south, and slowly, voluptuously apply that secret weapon—the bombshell's best friend—*lipstick*.

Last, but never least, give your mane a good shake, cloak yourself in a veil of perfume (if permitted at your location), and give yourself one last flirty, knowing look in the mirror. *Unstoppable!*

Now get back out there.

Sprinkle Stardust Wherever You Go

As you promenade through the corridors and cubicles, hold the belief that every person you see is making eye contact that is attentive and sincere, each word from you is well received, and everything you hear is pleasing in some way. Smile graciously. Go about your business. You've got this day in the palm of your silken hand.

But wait…how, exactly, has this magnificent creature suddenly appeared where once there was a crumpled grump of stiffly anxious angst? By taking a Beauty Break, *mes amours*. By purposefully reclaiming the confidence that is your birthright. By worshipping at the temple of your own sensuality. These tiny spells of time are essential to our wellbeing, as much as any lifestyle practice we adopt. Living well, aging well, *being* well, and, yes, looking fantastic at any age are all contingent upon a holistic approach. Those oft-repeated pieces of advice about clean eating, exercise, rest, meditation, fresh air, play? We say them ad nauseam *because they work*. Not only is claiming space in your day to take care of yourself decidedly un-frivolous, but it is an integral part of the bigger picture.

Who *doesn't* have job stress, after all? The true beauty of this ritual is that it can be embraced whenever and wherever you are, be it as a bustling professional, an artist balancing an income, or an at-home parent. We all have our hands full. Five minutes of adoring yourself with the added benefits of meditative breath and a mini-massage? Glowing like you just had a secret lunchtime tryst? A mind that is now clear and entirely peaceful? Well worth the time. Vain and silly? Not a chance. And the magickal benefits need no explanation. If the Witch is powerful, so is her sorcery. If she's dragging, her potency wanes. It's time to reclaim yourself. Whatever are you waiting for, beauty?

Alise Marie *is an actress, writer, and certified holistic nutritionist. She is passionate about a plant-powered, eco-friendly lifestyle aligned with the cycles of nature, the moon, and the stars. She has been creating health and beauty potions for over thirty years, drawing from ancient traditions, herbalism, astrology, and tarot. Alise has been featured internationally in magazines, websites, and live events. She is also a contributor to* Enchanted Living *magazine, which presents her monthly online column "The Beauty Witch." She recently launched an eco-luxe beauty collection available at thebeautywitch.com.*

Illustrator: Bri Hermanson

Putting the Nature Back in Nature Spirituality

A.C. Fisher Aldag

Many Witches, Pagans, Wiccans, and other magick users often self-identify as practicing a form of nature spirituality. This usually means holding a reverence for nature, interacting with natural objects and entities as a personal spiritual practice, honoring the spirits and beings that dwell in nature, and stewarding our Earth. It can include worship of Nature as an entity with a consciousness, represented by a deity such as Gaia. It can also mean a nontheistic practice that connects an individual with our natural world.

However, in the course of our busy lives, we sometimes find we are disconnected from our natural environment. We might work indoors, dwell in a home with central air conditioning and heating, and commute by motor vehicle. Our interaction with nature might be limited to taking ten steps from our apartment to our car. A person who lives on the seventeenth floor of a condominium in a major metropolitan area might feel that it's difficult to cultivate a relationship with nature. This article explores ways that even the busiest city dweller can enjoy some spiritual practices that connect with nature.

I'm immersed in nature every day. When I was young, in a scouting program I was called the "Nature Nut" when I picked up spiders and snakes to remove from our cabin. Currently I live in the country, surrounded by forests and wetlands. Our family grows much of our own food. Deer, rabbits, wild turkeys, frogs, raccoons, opossums, and dozens of bird species dwell in our yard. During summer nights, the sky is lit by fireflies (lightning bugs) and abuzz with the sound of katydids. There are a score of tree species and hundreds of other flora. I realize that not everyone is able to surround themselves with nature. However, opportunities abound for those who live in suburbs and even cities to foray into the natural world—or bring nature indoors—in small yet meaningful ways.

Short but Sweet Connections with Nature

Let's begin with simple ways that Witches with busy lives can make an appointment with nature. Of course, that starts with getting outdoors! It doesn't have to be an hours-long hike. On your lunch break or after your daily obligations, venture outside. First we'll state the obvious: please wear sunscreen and organic insect repellent to make your experience more pleasurable. Also remember to hydrate.

Locate a greenspace near your workplace or school. During your lunch break, have a picnic or take a short walk outside. Look for five different species of birds, five different trees or plants, and five other natural things such as insects, stones, pinecones, berries, acorns, feathers, or leaves. Seek tiny flowers among the grasses. Are any tenacious plants growing between cracks in the cement? Leave a small, meaningful offering beneath a rock or at the base of a tree, like a crystal or a handful of birdseed. Stare at the sky, count the clouds, enjoy the different colors. Speak words of power, such as "I appreciate my natural world" or "I'm connected with spirits of nature." Journal what you've seen and look up their magickal significance. A crow can be a messenger from the spirit world, a squirrel represents tenaciousness, and a star-shaped flower can symbolize the four directions and spirit.

Ground yourself by placing your feet flat on the earth, and feel the energies of the land. Slip off your shoes (if it's safe). Take deep breaths. Concentrate on drawing up power and releasing things like tension and worry. If you feel comfortable, chant the name of a spiritual entity or the four elements, or something like "I am one with the land." Scott Cunningham wrote a beautiful poem in his *Book of Shadows: The Path of an American Traditionalist*:

Wind, wind, guard thy kin,
Flame, flame, do not maim,
Rain, rain, leave amain,
Earth, earth, guard my worth.

The entire poem was intended as a protection rite against a storm, but those lines can be used as a chant to appreciate nature.

Cultivate a Relationship with Nature

Another way to interact with our environment is to take an hour or two and visit a produce farm, arboretum, beach, aquarium, hiking trail, or a local, state, or national park. We probably think of places like

Yellowstone National Park or Lake Michigan as being "nature," but we might not consider our backyard or a roadside rest area as having that same status. Yet of course they do! If you go monthly to a place, take note of seasonal changes. Did some of the birds migrate? What flowers are blooming? Do the plants have seedpods? These observations can align you with the seasonal holidays.

Lie on a blanket underneath the spreading branches of a tree. Look up at the undersides of the leaves. Are there birds or mammals? What is the wind saying? If it's legal where you live, gather shells, fallen leaves, stones, or wildflowers. Arrange these on your altar for a longer-lasting relationship with nature. Or take pictures! Seek auguries in the clouds or in found objects. Seeds can increase abundance, pink stones symbolize love, and dandelions equate with sunshine and wishes. Search for aquatic life in a stream or pond—minnows, turtles, frogs, snails, and plants unique to a wetland. Take a pet for a walk, or bring them outdoors in a carrier.

Seek auguries in the clouds or in found objects. Seeds can increase abundance, pink stones symbolize love, and dandelions equate with sunshine and wishes.

A field guide can help you identify the plants growing in roadside ditches or community greenspaces, or check online. Then put away your phone and enjoy all the beauty that surrounds you. Look for mushrooms (although don't touch), tree bark, the many-colored stones in the gravel, or common birds such as sparrows, pigeons, and starlings. What direction are they flying? Look up some oracles and omens related to birds, plants, and trees.

Nature can be appreciated even in inclement weather. Venture into the snow or rain and gather some in a bowl for use as moon water (a liquid charged with intent under a full moon for magickal use). Bathe your face with the water or use it to anoint ritual tools such as a chalice or crystal. Step outside at night. What insects or birds do you hear stirring? Can you see any constellations? What phase is the moon in? Reach out with your mind to connect to spirits, deities, or simply the heartbeat of the Earth.

Visit a nature center, conservation club, or park interpretive center. These locations often have displays of rehabilitated birds, up close and personal; the fur and cast footprints of large mammals; or snakes and other reptiles, safely behind glass. Some nature centers have windows at feeding stations where birds and mammals are eating their lunch. If you have space at your home, create your own feeding station: suet for woodpeckers; thistle or nyjer seed for finches; corn for jays, crows, squirrels, and chipmunks; uncolored sugar water for hummingbird and bee feeders; greens for rabbits or hedgehogs; and birdseed for everyone else. Put up nesting boxes. Ask birds to carry messages to ancestors or spirits. These activities are fun for children and seniors as well, so you can connect to loved ones as you connect to nature.

Travel in Natural Beauty

If you're stuck in the car, you can still interact with nature. Take "the road less traveled." One time on our way from Detroit to Cleveland, we drove along the marshy areas near Lake Erie. There we saw wetland flowers, muskrat houses, egrets, herons, ospreys, and even a bald eagle nest. Many roadside rest areas have short hiking trails and scenic overlooks to view rock formations, river gorges, and foothills. Roll down the windows and inhale the scent of the land.

Check out plants in deserts, swamps, or jungle areas. Enjoy lunch at a roadside picnic table. Touch your palms to a tree. Acknowledge the Earth, Sea, and Sky, the traditional three worlds of Celtic people. Tell the natural world that you appreciate its gifts of beauty.

Summertime brings a multitude of Earth religious festivals, which can include shopping at metaphysical vendors, workshops and rituals, and opportunities to enjoy nature: bonfires, drum circles, walks, herb identification classes, outdoor yoga and meditation, etc. Many festivals include camping in a safe environment outdoors during both daylight and nighttime. Autumn means Pagan Pride Days. Check online for nearby gatherings.

Guardians of the Planet

Next we'll move on to stewarding our Earth. Search for products that are ethically sourced, organic, and produced using resource conservation. (*Organic* means produced using only natural ingredients.) Try to find items that are made from renewable materials. (*Renewable* means replaceable in a timely manner, like toilet paper made from hemp rather than old-growth hardwoods.) Shop at merchants who have a commitment to preserving our environment. Search for groceries at farmers' markets or "you pick" farms. Whisper affirmations as you shop, such as "I'll find the most delicious, beneficial goodies at the best price!"

An excursion to a local farmstead for berries or vegetables can be a fun holiday/sabbat activity for a coven or family. While you're there, look for wild and domestic animals, birds, and insects. How many different plants can you spot? Don't forget the best part—eating! Make an offering of foods to spiritual beings. Thank the entities for their contribution. Affirm/speak magick into being while enjoying the food with words such as these: "As I eat these locally grown carrots, I feel my body becoming healthier."

Try to reduce waste, including things tossed in the trash. If you have space, compost organic waste, including coffee grounds, tea bags, vegetable and fruit peels, rinds and cores, and leftovers that don't contain meat. Keep compost in a sealed bucket until it can be removed to a compost pile. Find out if your municipality has a recycling program or if there is a local drop-off center. If not, perhaps bring up this matter to a governing body, or look for private recycling companies.

Buy recycled products. (*Recycled* means that the object is undergoing its second or more use. Labels indicate what percentage of recycled material is contained in the product.) Some areas recycle old tires, paint, and electronics several times a year. Community centers that collect old clothes aren't just looking to repurpose designer fashions; worn-out clothing is used to create fiberfill and paper. A coven or family can recycle things such as printer ink cartridges, old computers, eyeglasses, medicine bottles, and soda pop cans. (Make sure you have an outlet before collecting a garage full of stuff!) As these activities commence, make affirmations about connecting to our Earth. Here are some ideas: "Every time I wear this jacket made from recycled plastic bottles, I reaffirm my relationship with Nature." "I cast off things that no longer serve my purpose. May this object find a beneficial use."

One step further in conservation is performing a trash cleanup for Earth Day or on a holiday/sabbat. Many locations offer a highway tidying program where they provide garbage bags and actually dispose of the trash you pick up. Some parks or beaches have organized cleanup days. This is a fantastic opportunity for an Earth religious group. It's gratifying to see a sign proclaiming "This highway sponsored by the New Moon Witchcraft Coven." If you're a solitary practitioner, consider joining a local service club involved with environmental preservation.

Backyard Blessings

Homeowners have many opportunities to celebrate nature, including mundane acts such as mowing the lawn, pulling weeds, and transplanting flowers. Planting a garden rewards us with food, herbs, and flowers, which can attract beneficial insects, such as butterflies, and birds, including lovely, darting hummingbirds. Nothing is quite so grounding as digging in the dirt! Gardening connects us with the turning seasons and is a wonderful way to celebrate the sabbats.

A garden doesn't have to be a huge plot with every type of vegetable and a hundred species of flowers, and we need not own land to plant a few seeds. Apartment dwellers can cultivate, too. A garden can be a row of sunflowers along the side of a building, crocus and daffodil bulbs that appear each spring, succulents in a pot in a sunny window, a colorful flower bed, a grapevine on an arbor, pots of flowers or veggies on a balcony, a fruit tree, or replacing a grass lawn with a few raised beds of edible flowers, herbs, and plants that don't spread much, including peppers, dwarf tomatoes, salad greens, potatoes, and other root crops. Some farms, universities, and government agencies offer garden space rental or fun things like "pick your own blueberry bush." For a small fee, the farmworkers water and care for your area, then you harvest it at the appropriate time.

Garden spaces can be decorated with stones and crystals, wind chimes, statuary representing deities and spirit beings such as fairies, and a bench for sitting and contemplating nature. Protect a large garden from hungry wildlife with old, discarded wooden pallets repurposed into an attractive rustic fence. (First check with landlords, city officials, and homeowner associations.) Instead of using chemical pesticides and herbicides, find organic ways of removing harmful insects and undesirable plants. Vinegar kills weeds growing in the cracks of a sidewalk or concrete foundation. A mixture of castile soap and a few drops of hot pepper juice sprayed on leaves can repel bugs. The compost mentioned earlier can be contained in a commercial vessel or piled inside four wooden pallets wired together in a square. Compost (also sometimes called mulch) should be kept damp and turned over often with a pitchfork. The resulting rich, black earth is a source of natural fertilizer.

Many people who live in apartments garden indoors, producing houseplants, flowers, small vegetables, and culinary or medicinal herbs. A windowsill garden can be magickal, with green growing plants in colorful pots, tiny statuettes, glass baubles, and a wee bit of soil from our sacred Earth to sustain life. Earthenware pots can also harbor crystals or stones found on a beach and be the receptacle for ashes from an incense burner or items you desire to "earth." Houseplants produce oxygen and give a sense of groundedness. Plants grown indoors will need water and fertilizer, and it doesn't hurt to talk or sing to them. Grow lights can help provide enough artificial sunshine during the winter months. Involve your plant allies in ceremonies such as representing the element of earth or north, or using a living holly plant for Yuletide symbolism.

Creating Community

A community garden is a great way to meet other people and to grow food for group members or a charitable organization. All it takes is a small plot of arable land, some seeds, a water source, and a few volunteers. Check with homeowner associations, government bodies (such as a parks and rec committee), civic clubs, assisted living facilities, schools, and religious organizations to request space for a community garden. A big empty yard is perfect and reduces the amount of lawn-mowing required. Some Pagan groups have established land sanctuaries, which can support a garden. Tools such as shovels, hoes, and rakes can be shared. Larger tools, such as a rototiller, can often be rented from a hardware store. A farmer might offer to till the earth for the first time (look in your local shopping guide or on bulletin boards at farm supply stores). Fundraising for your community garden is also an excellent way to meet people and to do an interfaith project.

Some cities have other types of gardens, such as a historic garden, which contains only the plants grown during a certain era. A rain garden is a place that has layers of rocks, gravel, and sand, and plants that can absorb the runoff from city streets and filter out toxins such as road salt. The rain garden often needs tending, such as removing non-beneficial weeds or debris that washes into it from the street. A wildlife garden is a place that sustains beneficial insects, birds, and animals. It might contain berry bushes, plants such as milkweed for endangered monarch butterflies, flowers for pollinators like bees and bats, and trees that produce seeds and nuts to help sustain birds, squirrels, and other mammals. Check with museums, nature centers, arboretums, or conservation clubs about establishing and maintaining a special garden.

Everyday Nature Spirituality

Those who are physically able can take visits to nature one step further by entering a marathon or bike rally, visiting a cavern, or walking down a hundred steps to view a waterfall. For those of us not quite so athletically inclined, we take nature where we find her. Set up a lawn chair outside of your front door. Look out the window at a thunderstorm. Raise your hands to the sky at midnight and sing a song.

Honor the Goddess as Ceres, Bhumi, Demeter, Terra, Prithvi, Hertha, Pachamama, Diana, Houtu, or Danu. Invoke the God as Cernunnos/Herne/the Bucca, Geb, Amaethon, Tudigong, Veles, or Osiris. Express gratitude to trees for our oxygen. Touch your hands to the ground and mindfully connect with the earth currents. Speak intentions into manifestation at a natural liminal time, such as dawn or the Autumnal Equinox (Mabon, Alban Elfed), or in a liminal place, like the edge of a ravine or at the shore.

Benedythion (Blessed be)!

A.C. Fisher Aldag (*Bangor, Michigan*) *has been practicing a folkloric tradition of nature spirituality for over forty years. She presents classes and workshops on basic witchcraft for beginners, British Isles magickal traditions, folkplays, ritual drumming, inclusivity for the differently-abled, and fun artsy-craftsy stuff. A.C. lives near the shores of beautiful Lake Michigan. She is the author of* Common Magick: Origins and Practices of British Folk Magick, *available from Llewellyn.*

Illustrator: Tim Foley

Practical Divination Journaling

Blake Octavian Blair

Wise magical practitioners sing the praises of journaling for spiritual purposes. They say we should develop a regular journaling practice and faithfully adhere to it. A huge number of well-written books by authors with genuine expertise ask this of their readers. After all, the most helpful learning is often done in active engagement. However, I know what you are thinking when such a request is made: that it sounds daunting, and forming new habits is hard. I hear you. You're not alone. The good news is that the suggestion

likely wasn't meant to be daunting or hard. Further, it truly doesn't have to be.

One form of journaling that I have made a regular practice, and that I think could help you find a window into a regular spiritual journaling practice, is divination journaling. In this article I'm going to share my easy guidelines and journaling format that will hopefully pave the road ahead for an enjoyable regular divination journaling practice for anyone with the desire.

It took me years, with several fits and starts, to find a format and philosophy of divination journaling that worked for me. To get going on any new undertaking, one naturally needs motivation and drive. The upshot of divination journaling is that its practicality is a built-in motivator. We all want the practical heads-up and insight that we can glean from a quick reading. However, the full potential of its practical usefulness is lost when we pull a card and it's forgotten about the next day. That is where journaling comes in.

Another way to make the experience enjoyable, so that you actually look forward to journaling, is to choose a blank journal that is attractive to you. Tastes vary widely, so find something that appeals to you, that you like the tactile feel of, and that looks inviting. My own is a brown suede leather journal with a pentagram inside some Celtic knotwork embossed on the cover.

The next step is, of course, to employ your favorite divination deck or tool, whether it be tarot, oracle cards, rune stones, or ogham staves, etc. If you have an attraction and connection to the tool, you'll look forward to using it. Of course, this journaling technique is also a good way to explore and learn a new deck or tool and become familiar with how it speaks to you. You also do not have to use the same deck or tool every single time you engage in divination journaling, and I accounted for and addressed that in the design of my journaling format, which we will explore in short order.

Developing Good Journaling Habits

Now let's discuss a little about how to form the habit and how often one should journal. I find that when people want to undertake a new regular practice, they often set themselves up for failure. Many people feel the need to achieve unwavering perfection. They set their expectations extremely high, to something virtually impossible, instead of setting achievable goals.

> **[Many people] set their expectations extremely high, to something virtually impossible, instead of setting achievable goals. I'm in favor of allowing a bit of flexibility for success.**

I'm in favor of allowing a bit of flexibility for success. I don't feel the beginning goal should be an in-depth daily divination and critical analysis. If you're new to divination journaling, you might like to try something more achievable, like a Monday, Wednesday, Friday divination schedule, or even just once a week if that seems to fit better in your life. You get to set the schedule, and you're allowed to be flexible with it. If you miss a day, pick up again on the next round, or just do your divination when you have time. Falling out of habit is not a crime; not restarting and continuing on would be the crime. You're also allowed to decide that a journaling plan or frequency you tried just doesn't work for you, and you can try on a different plan for size and see how that works. That isn't failure at all. In fact, it can be considered a success, as you're finding out what does and does not work for you. This process is an experiment!

Once you've gathered a blank journal and a divination deck or tool that inspires you, it is almost time to get down to the business of actually divining. Before beginning, as part of the consecration process for the journal, I like to inscribe on the first page a prayer, incantation, or sigil as a blessing. Pick something that speaks to you or is from your tradition. I think this is a nice touch and effectively serves to begin the work ahead. And with that, you are ready to begin your first divination journaling session.

The ritual of actually performing the reading can be as elaborate as you wish, but you won't need much space, even for the cards and tools, as I have designed this format to be for single-card readings. Whether you'd like to say a prayer, light a candle, burn some incense, or cast a circle is up to you. I suggest you have a ritual of some kind, but keep it simple. Rituals need not be elaborate to be magical and effective, and they are also easier to perform on a regular basis or on the fly when you keep them simple.

Rituals need not be elaborate to be magical and effective, and they are also easier to perform on a regular basis or on the fly when you keep them simple.

A note about timing: many people seem to think that to do a daily divination, they need to perform it first thing in the morning to start their day. This isn't true, and I almost never do. I'm not a morning person and never have been! I normally perform my divination journaling session sometime in the early afternoon after lunch. You could simply hold the intention that the period covered by the reading runs from early afternoon to early afternoon. An interesting historical fact is that the traditional Celtic day is seen as running from sundown to sundown. So don't feel pressed to have to spring from bed and attempt this exercise before your morning tea or coffee.

Formatting the Journal

I use one page per reading and generally do a reading to reflect the next twenty-four hours. I've found that works well for me. I started with the goal of doing it daily, but then adjusted to a few days a week instead. I find I still often end up doing it more than a few days a week, but a daily reading is an obtainable goal that I allow flexibility with. (You'll hear me talk a lot about flexibility.)

I begin each reading by putting the date in the upper left-hand corner of the page and the current moon phase in the upper right-hand corner. Next, under the date at the left, I write what deck (or tool) I am using. I do not exclusively use one deck in my divination journaling, so this is a useful notation since different decks have a habit of "speaking" differently. Under the title of the deck, I record the name of the card I drew. Then I begin recording my interpretation of the message from the card drawn.

Under the name of the card drawn, I write "Initial Reading" and then record my thoughts, impressions, and interpretations of the message of the card. Usually this is a mere three to five sentences. I find that keeping it to a short paragraph helps me zero in on the important highlights of the messages to me for the coming day.

The next section of the journal page, which I place under the "Initial Reading," is one I title "Keywords." Here I place bullet-pointed keywords and phrases or perhaps notate extra information like influences of animal energies present on particular cards, etc. I include things that stick out as pertinent to me individually or are classic associations of the card I want to highlight in relation to the message and be reminded of later.

After the "Keywords," the final section I put on the page of each reading is one I title "Reflection." I fill out this section at the end of the designated reading forecast, for example, the day after the divination session. If it's been more than twenty-four hours since the reading, that is okay; I just note the date next to the heading of the reflection. Here I record how things actually panned out and compare the reading to the life events that transpired. This, again, is usually a short paragraph about equal in size to that of the "Initial Reading." It is the combination of the "Initial Reading" and the "Reflection" that is of real practical use over time. Many people seem to journal their divinations but never record how they compare to what transpired in life afterward. Thus, I felt it important to build in a "Reflection" session to my divination journaling format.

A bonus section I sometimes add at the bottom of the page after the "Reflection" is a "Gratitude" section. When we reflect, sometimes we have pleasant things to report and sometimes we have less than pleasant things to record that have transpired. Stand-alone gratitude journaling is never something that took for me, but some days I find it is helpful to add a few bullet points of things that happened over the past day that I was grateful for. This seems to work for me as an add-on practice to divination journaling.

Flex for Success

Now that we've taken a walk through the basic structure of my divination journaling format, I'm going to revisit the importance of flexibility. Do I divination journal every day? No, I do not. Do you have to? No, you do not. Do I keep a strict schedule for my readings? Actually, no, I do not. It is useful to be diligent at the outset if you can in order to form the habit. Once the habit is truly formed, it's easier to miss a session or take a break and return to the habit. But I feel that if you're too rigid in your expectations and you're hard on yourself about it, you won't maintain the practice.

I tend to divination journal three days a week on average, so it is what I'd term a regular practice. You will notice in my walk-through so far that I have built in little ways to adapt the format so that it is clear and concise and allows flexibility. You can switch decks and not be confused later on with your recorded readings, as you always record the deck or tool you used. Different decks speak differently and have unique voices. The "Keywords" section is really useful here and allows you to record unique messages and associations. The "Reflection" can really be done at any point after the reading. Just note the date on which you did it, so you know how much time passed while the events you recorded were transpiring. And honestly, if you fall out of habit and want to pick it back up again, and you didn't write a reflection for your last reading and you do not remember what happened relating to the card, simply date the Reflection section and then write "No Reflection" and move on, performing your next reading and starting your next journal page. Don't beat yourself up. Just begin again.

I find that this format makes the practice both functional and achievable. The best part is that after you complete your first journal page, you're successful. You'll have done a reading, journaled your interpretations, and then reflected upon them after the period you've read for has passed and notated how the events unfolded and relate to your reading. Success is achieved with every completed page, and then the next blank page beckons you to your next successful journaling effort. You will also have the cumulative success of being able to observe trends over time, and further, because you are notating the moon phase, you can begin to relate that to your interpretations and actions, and start to form associations in relation to the moon over time.

While this format focuses on divination, my hope is that you can adapt it to expand your journaling efforts to other spiritual practices as well. For example, you could keep a meditation journal, where you change the deck and card notations to the type of meditation you're using and your meditative goal or intention. Then you adapt the content of "Initial Reading" to record the messages and experiences you had in meditation, and "Reflection" is a reflection of how those messages relate to real-life events. This is just one example.

Another possibility is a dream journal. When adapting this format, I always recommend notating the moon phase, as it often seems to add an extra nugget of insight. For a dream journal, you could notate the date you had the dream and your initial thoughts on the dream, and notate key symbols or themes in bullet points where "Keywords" would be. Then later you could write a reflection about anything that unfolded in your waking reality.

Regular spiritual practices do not have to be static and unbending; flexibility can be the key to success. It was a number of years before I began spiritual journaling on any topic on a regular basis, and I have found this divination journaling format a successful tool for getting pen to hand and returning to the page. I hope you do as well. May you experience and observe many blessings as you record the magic unfolding in your life!

Blake Octavian Blair *is a Druid and shamanic practitioner, ordained minister, writer, Usui Reiki Master-Teacher, and musical artist. He incorporates mystical traditions from both the East and West with a reverence for the natural world into his own brand of spirituality. Blake holds a degree in English and religion from the University of Florida. He is an avid reader, knitter, crafter, and member of the Order of Bards, Ovates & Druids (OBOD). He loves communing with nature and exploring its beauty, whether it is within the city or while hiking in the woods. Blake lives in the New England region of the US with his beloved husband. Visit him on the web at www.blakeoctavianblair.com.*

Illustrator: Bri Hermanson

Relating with Your Home & Plants for a Greater Sense of Spiritual Connection

Durgadas Allon Duriel

I think few topics are more important in spiritual writing than how to foster a greater sense of spiritual connectedness and alignment. For many of us, the moments when we feel connected are among the richest in our lives, and a large part of our motivation for embarking upon a spiritual path. And yet, they are often just that—moments. But they needn't be. Through time-tested practices, we can come to a more abiding sense of spiritual connectedness and alignment in our everyday lives. Here, I will share some practices that helped me

do that in my life—namely, cultivating a conscious relationship with my home and the plants in my home and neighborhood—after first exploring how they came to me.

Connecting with My Home

While the concept of forming a relationship with plants has been part of my spiritual outlook since childhood, the notion of doing it with my home and the items in it was new to me as of a few years ago. I'd read about animism before—generally defined as the attribution of spirits to inanimate objects—but never adopted it in the literal sense. What I believed, which was reflective of my training, was that all things possess a divine essence: everything in the Universe is cut from the same sacred cloth and, by virtue of that, holy. While this belief has many virtues and is beautiful (and I still hold it), in practice it can have the effect of equating everything in a manner that waters down distinctions. When we focus solely on the essence, and the essence of all things is shared, it is harder to appreciate the holy value of distinctions and to be in relationship with those distinctions.

Consequently, the notion of connecting with the particular spirit of things—like my home, my bed, my favorite chair—wasn't what I was taught or inclined to do. Starting around 2019 though, I began seeing the work of neo-animistic teachers on social media. Their content piqued my interest and planted a seed in my consciousness, but I didn't act on it. A year or two later, I started listening to a guided meditation each morning from Louise Hay that involved gratitude, including thanking the items in our home. This seemed like an apt moment to begin that practice, so I started doing it.

The practice was very simple: I would touch or kiss the walls of my home and say thank you. I would touch the stove and thank it for its role in my life, thank my favorite chair while sitting in it, thank my toilet and express gratitude for modern plumbing, and so on.

At first, the main thing I noticed about this practice was that it felt good. With consistent repetition over time though, I observed it deepening. A warm vibe began emanating from my home, and I recognized that I enjoyed being in it more. Rather than feeling isolated or sequestered while the Covid pandemic raged on, I began to feel safely contained. A little after that, something dawned on me that reinforced the value of this practice: I didn't feel lonely when I was in my home by myself. This isn't to suggest that I didn't miss human companionship. I did, especially during the more isolated stretches of the pandemic. But I didn't feel alone. I felt surrounded by comforting presences in a way that I never had before.

> At first, the main thing I noticed about this practice was that it felt good....A warm vibe began emanating from my home, and I recognized that I enjoyed being in it more.

When I used to think of animism, the part that always tripped me up was what I assumed to be the act of ascribing a human-like intelligence and spirit to inanimate objects, for example, making a broom out to be a kind of human-like being. What I have discovered instead, and this may be something that's best understood through experience rather than contemplating it, is that it's more like the broom has a broom-like personality, a broom-like spirit—not unlike how an animal has a different intelligence and personality from a human, yet clearly both of those qualities are there.

This led to a breakthrough that has aided me in opening to this new facet of my spiritual life: sacred relationship with objects. While still connecting with the divine essence and seeking that around me, I could also form a relationship with the individual spirit of "things." The practice was a sort of spiritual both/and rather than an either/

or, and much like how a meaningful relationship with a person can lead to a greater connection with qualities like love, compassion, and centeredness, so can a meaningful connection with an "object." The dimension of relationship can facilitate connecting with divine essence, rather than proving to be a distraction from it. The trick, in my experience, is to hold that objective in mind while engaging in the actions of relationship.

After practicing this way for a few months, an amazing thing happened to me. I was walking through my apartment one day and felt a strong message to buy an air purifier. The odd thing about this was that I already had one, but the message was clear, and interestingly it felt like it was coming from my apartment. "Okay," I thought, and I ordered one later that day. At the time I took this as a sign that my apartment, which I now felt affectionately connected to, was creating a healthier living environment for me so I could stay in it, as I'd had some issues with it in the past. When the purifier arrived, I set it up so that both rooms of my apartment would have clean air.

The next day, there was a fire in my apartment building on the floor below mine. It raged to where that floor was completely destroyed, and while the fire didn't reach my floor, the floor filled with smoke. Because of the air purifiers in my apartment, items that would've likely been permanently damaged by smoke were salvageable. The new purifier came at just the right time, and I felt like that was the spirit of my home's way of caring for me and also saying goodbye, as the building then became uninhabitable.

Practice: Cultivating a Sacred Relationship with Your Home

The practice of cultivating a conscious, sacred relationship with my home that I learned and continue to perform is so simple. It's just a matter of expressing gratitude. Once a day or so, kiss or affectionately touch the walls of your home and say thank you, unless you are in an emotional state where that would feel unhealthy or phony. Offer thanks that you have shelter, something countless ancestors of ours didn't have, at least not to the degree that most of us do now. Then thank your appliances and the furniture in your home. If you live in a big home, you may want to divide this up based on different days (e.g., thanking your kitchen on Sunday, your living room on Monday, etc.). But I wouldn't let more than a day go by without thanking your home itself, unless you don't feel up for that. Then watch what happens!

Connecting with the Plants in My Neighborhood

When I was a child, the backyard in my family home felt like a forest. Though to an adult it was no more than a large, tree-lined yard, to a five-year-old it may as well have been the Hundred Acre Wood. My love of plants and sense of spiritual connection to the earth began there, and that earth-centered approach has been one of the mainstays of my spiritual path throughout the years. Learning about the goddess Gaia and the archetype of Mother Nature was actually my first draw into paganism, building off those early experiences with the "woods." That said, my actual practice of engaging with Nature has waxed and waned, with certain threshold experiences that made me feel more connected to Nature and thus more spiritually connected in general.

In my early twenties, I had the good fortune to participate in an intensive spiritual training program located on a ranch in Southern California. Every Sunday we would spend ten to twelve hours doing projects on the property, most of which involved the land. I had the blessing to harvest plants directly from the hillside, pick fruit from the orchards, clip herbs from huge bushes of them, and even plant and maintain a small herb garden. While engaging in this week after week alongside studying and practicing ritual and meditation intensively, I noticed something shifting in my relationship to plants. I began to perceive a presence or consciousness emanating from them.

At first, this was subtle, but by the end of my time with the program, I felt the presence of plants so strongly that it was difficult to ignore. Additionally, this presence was spiritually nourishing to me to a profound degree. I like to say that plants speak to us in a language that helps us come home within ourselves, and that is what my experience of plant consciousness was like. I learned much of what I know about spiritual connection and alignment from tuning in to trees and various other plants.

I felt the presence of plants so strongly that it was difficult to ignore. [It] was spiritually nourishing to me to a profound degree. I like to say that plants speak to us in a language that helps us come home within ourselves.

In my late thirties, I found myself making my home in a dense city, which was a surprise to me, as I'd always imagined myself moving to a more rural area as I got older, in light of how much I love Nature. I would walk to the store and my other errands, sometimes remarking to myself that while I enjoyed city life, I didn't like feeling so detached from Nature. As much as this city felt like home, how could this be where I would end up settling down?

Then one day I took a cue from my practice of thanking the items in my home and started greeting the plants in my neighborhood. This greeting was very simple. I'd tune in to their energy, as I had done for years, and sort of offer friendly vibes to them. Similar to what had happened with my home, as I practiced this consistently, I felt more and more connected when I was walking around the city I lived in. In time, I stopped feeling disconnected from Nature.

This isn't to say that I don't feel more connected when I'm in a grove or park—I do. But now, I feel far more connected where I am, and that changed even more once I established an indoor garden in my home that I could greet each day. As with thanking the items in my home and my home itself, this practice has made me feel far less lonely. It has also become my way of connecting with the land where I live.

Practice: Communing with Plants

The practice I use for communing with plants is fairly straightforward, though it may take some solid practice to get a handle on it. Also, it may be best to practice this outdoors surrounded by a large number of plants or trees rather than with something like a houseplant. This is because, in my experience, the presence is louder in those conditions. That said, you can certainly try this with a houseplant, particularly if that is the only realistic option available to you.

Here are the steps:

1. Sit or stand before a plant.

2. Close your eyes and feel the presence within yourself.

3. Open your eyes and focus on the plant. Try to feel the parallel presence within it. This is the same as what you would do if you were trying to feel the presence within a human being, like after hugging someone or kissing them or just while making eye contact.

4. Offer warm, nurturing thoughts to the plant as you do this.

5. Simply notice what you feel. Allow yourself to relax and enter a semi-trance state if you can, just being present to what is.

It may take some time for this practice to be effective, but I believe that if you persist with it, you are likely to get solid results.

The Joy of Relationship

One of the most beautiful aspects of these practices for me is the way that spiritual connection is sought in what is here, on this Earth, now. While I'm not disparaging working with the unseen world, I find something beautiful in seeking the spiritual in what is before me. We don't have to go anywhere other than where we are now to connect and form meaningful spiritual relationships. The divine is right here, and the entire world is inspirited. This can be revealed to us not through abstraction, but through simple acts like saying thank you or hello, and having the humility to let go of notions of being superior to the inanimate or assuming we know what its limitations are. We don't have to go anywhere other than where we are to connect and form meaningful spiritual relationships.

Durgadas Allon Duriel (San Francisco, CA) *is a licensed clinical social worker and a certified holistic health practitioner working in private practice. He is also an astrologer, yogi, and magic worker, having practiced magic since childhood and eventually discovering modern paganism and Wicca in high school and later initiating into a Hermetic order in 2005. He trained there intensively for two and a half years, focusing on astrology, Kabbalah, Yoga, tarot, and ritual, which he continues to study and practice. He holds a master's degree in social welfare from UCLA.*

Illustrator: Tim Foley

Channeling with Cannabis

Kerri Connor

I began channeling long before I understood what channeling was.

My first experience came when I was only six years old and knew that my family dog had passed away before anyone came to tell me. How did I know? The guy who was in a bunch of photographs around my house told me that she had died and he was there to take her with him.

As that same six-year-old child, the houses I went to—relatives who lived next door and in the next house down from that—all had the same black and white photo of this young, white,

dark-haired man. I always assumed it was a picture of Jesus. In my mind, Jesus had stopped by to pick up my dog and take her to heaven, not an unreasonable belief for a six-year-old raised in a Christian faith.

Two years later, when my mother passed away, I saw her on the night of her funeral, standing at the foot of my bed. Soon after her death, the photographs of the young man I had thought was Jesus came down in my house. When I asked my aunt why my dad was taking down the Jesus pictures, she explained that the pictures weren't of Jesus; they were of a brother of mine who died before I was a twinkle in my daddy's eye. It took me a few more years to realize the meaning of that sentiment. (I could go into the whole trauma of learning about being a replacement baby, but that would be an entirely different article!)

This told me that the man who had come to me about my dog was not Jesus but instead my brother. My dead brother. With this knowledge, combined with the experience of my mother coming to see me the night we buried her, I concluded that we (as in everyone) could still communicate with people after they died. When I pointed this out to the minister at our church, however, I was quickly corrected that this was not something everyone did, and those who did were seen as evil. I locked my skills away, with no attempt to use them for another eight years.

Denial is a powerful tool, and if I had any other encounters before the age of sixteen, I don't remember them. I had locked myself down from being able to communicate with spirits on my own for so long and so hard that I now had to use a tool, which could often result in me receiving garbled, unverifiable messages, if any at all. My tool of choice was a spirit board. Though I am highly skilled with this form of communication, it never became a regular part of my practices.

Given Another Chance

When I moved into my current home in 1999, I learned right away that there was a spirit attached to the house. He had died there of brain cancer, with his daughter (my husband's ex-wife) caring for him. When she moved out after his death, no one told him. He wandered the home looking for his daughter. It didn't help that this daughter and I have the same name but spelled differently. His presence was the first one I had felt so clearly in a long time.

After that experience, they began happening more frequently with more spirits. It was as if the walls had crumbled enough to let bits and pieces through. I was once again able to communicate with spirits without the use of any kind of go-between, but once again, the messages came through often garbled and unintelligible.

While I was able to communicate again, I had absolutely no control over who showed up, or when or where. I couldn't stop them from coming, and I couldn't always successfully connect with who I wanted when I wanted. This became discouraging. Discouragement makes my walls go up, and my connections become even more erratic, which causes more discouragement, and another vicious cycle begins.

Once I began using cannabis for meditation, it quickly became clear how beneficial it could also be for channeling. Indica strains allow the mind to calm and let down the built-up walls that protect from unwanted intrusions. Sometimes those walls can be difficult to lower, but cannabis helps let them fall away. Then, when I want, they can easily be put back into place. Building the walls was never a problem for me, but their sturdy construction made lowering them an issue. I decided it was finally time for me to hone my channeling skills and began using cannabis to help guide me into, through, and out of channeling sessions.

Not only does cannabis lower walls, but it also helps us focus where we want. This brings clarity to situations where we once found confusion and cloudiness. The entheogenic nature of cannabis allows us to connect with spirits, deities, and the universal All or One. This stronger, direct connection helps to provide more detailed messages for the recipient (whether the messages are for yourself or you are receiving them to deliver to other people). Cannabis works like the old radio dials used to select the correct frequency, giving us the clearest reception.

> **Cannabis allows us to connect with spirits, deities, and the universal All or One.... Cannabis works like the old radio dials used to select the correct frequency, giving us the clearest reception.**

Channeling has many practical purposes. I often use it to help me while I am writing, especially when I am looking for a different way to say or explain something. I can check in with my "writers' group" and instantly receive feedback with many different ideas. Living in a house with several ghosts present means channeling comes in handy and has made our pleasant coexistence under one roof possible. Over the years, I have delivered many messages, often of a medical nature, to friends from their deceased loved ones. I have been told sometimes when, and other times how, a person will die if they continue their current path. All these connections have been extremely useful and, in some cases, lifesaving.

It has been difficult to accept how important it is for me to actively practice channeling, but even I can no longer deny the results. As they say, the proof is in the pudding. Whereas I used to brush things off as coincidence or something everyone should have seen coming, I have learned over the years that these were excuses to not have confidence in myself and my skills. I have seldom been wrong with any of my predictions, but I always focused on the 2 percent of the time I was wrong about something, not the 98 percent of the time I was right—self-sabotage at its finest. Through shadow work and practice, I have learned to trust my abilities almost as much as those around me do. I am still a work in progress, as we all are.

When I first began to use cannabis with channeling, I approached it in much the same way I did with meditation. My first step was to get my mind into a quiet, receptive state through dosing and relaxing deep breathing. Once my mind was settled, I could then focus my attention on lowering my walls. It took considerable effort to bring them down. I soon learned that what I had envisioned in my mind as my "walls" was a vast simplification of the complex and intricate booby-trapped system I had built to protect myself from a bombardment I wasn't qualified to handle. My system had to be strong enough to keep out everything because there was so much to keep out.

Finding the Future

By the summer of 2019, I felt a distinctive change happening in the veil itself—or so I thought. Every year of my practice, I have kept track of when I start to feel the veil thin. Each year the date has moved earlier and earlier. It took a while, and lots of conversations with other witches, for me to realize it wasn't so much that the veil was thinning earlier, but instead, with my skills growing, that I was changing. The veil was disappearing for me because it was no longer a concern. By Yule of 2020, I realized the veil wasn't coming back. It no longer separates me from those who have passed on. I now slip much easier between this world and the next to communicate and channel with who I want or need to.

Though I had spent bursts of time on and off throughout the years working on channeling, it wasn't until I tried combining the path with cannabis that I found the perfect one for me to follow—a path that has increased my skills and brought its own sense of enlighten-ment. I now have far more confidence in my abilities and the results I receive.

While different people may receive varied types of messages, most of what I receive is related to the future—often in the form of a warn-ing or premonition of things to come—whether they are changeable or not. These messages have completely changed my outlook on life and the importance of preparing for the future. Premonitions led me to consider and choose new and interesting paths.

Exercise to Find Your Path

You, too, can use cannabis to lower your walls, calm your mind, and connect to the right frequencies to receive messages from beyond our plane of existence.

This beginning exercise helped me to begin my daily channeling practice. All you need is cannabis in your preferred method of con-sumption and a quiet spot to sit or lie down in comfortably to help you relax. You can set an alarm if you are concerned about falling asleep.

You, too, can use cannabis to lower your walls, calm your mind, and connect to the right frequencies to receive messages from beyond our plane of existence.

Take your cannabis in your preferred method to a good, comfortable high, and lie or sit down to relax with your eyes closed. Get as comfortable as possible. While you do this, focus on the thought of open-ing your mind to all possibilities. Open your mind to focus on what your senses detect all around you: What do you smell? Hear? Taste?

Do you see anything in your mind's eye? What do you feel in your immediate environment?

Paying attention to your environment through your senses is extremely important, because through this same process you will be able to better recognize shifts. These shifts may be signals of a connection that has been made. For example, when connecting with certain spirits, they may present with an identifier—such as the scent of a favorite perfume or a specific flower, or even the aroma of a favorite cookie recipe baking. Noticing these shifts announces their arrival.

Our sense of smell is often one of the first ways we recognize that a connection has been made with a loved one who has passed. It is a powerful sense that can immediately transfer us to a different time and place, as it pulls memories of the past and brings them into their own current existence.

As you focus on your senses, send out an invitation to whomever you want to connect with. Your invitation may be to a specific individual or to a defined group—whichever you choose. I highly suggest that your first communications be done with loved ones or ancestors. Since a connection to them already exists, they are easiest to call to, and to hear in return. They will also have so much to teach you. What you learn in your journeys with your ancestors will help you learn to communicate with others outside of your familiar realm.

Patience and focus are key. Working with cannabis increases both, providing another boost to your working. Be patient. You may not feel any connections the first few times. That's okay. Once you become more adept at feeling the shifts in energy with your senses, you'll find yourself making more and more connections before you know it.

Kerri Connor *is the author of* Spells for Good Times: Rituals, Spells, and Meditations to Boost Confidence & Positivity; CBD for Your Health, Mind, & Spirit; 420 Meditations: Enhance Your Spiritual

Practice with Cannabis; Wake, Bake & Meditate: Take Your Spiritual Practice to a Higher Level with Cannabis; *and* Spells for Tough Times. *Kerri leads the Gathering Grove, a registered 501(c)(3), family-friendly, eclectic pagan group. Visit her at KerriConnor.com.*

Illustrator: M. Kathryn Thompson

Witchcraft Essentials

PRACTICES, RITUALS & SPELLS

Boundary Setting for Witches

Melissa Tipton

Satisfying, healthy relationships require boundaries, but many of us were never taught how to set them, and in fact we might have grown up with the messaging that boundaries are rude, unkind, or just plain not allowed. So what's a witch to do? We're going to explore how personal boundaries are very much like the boundary of a witch's circle in order to understand how they support rather than detract from our relationships, and then we'll cover straightforward strategies for setting them.

The Benefits of Boundaries

First of all, what are boundaries? I define personal boundaries as the limits and rules that help us live in alignment with our values. This definition also helps clarify what boundaries are *not*—namely, boundaries aren't about controlling other people. Let's use an analogy to illustrate the difference. You're sitting in a room. This is your space, and within this space you get to set limits and rules regarding what happens here. Perhaps one of your rules is "Before entering, I need you to knock and wait for permission." You might also have rules that define how you can behave in the room (self-boundaries), such as "I can read and make art here, but I'm not allowed to throw trash on the floor."

Now, let's say your friend Kai is also sitting in their room a couple houses over. This is their personal space, and within it they're allowed to set limits and rules regarding how the space is used. If you go over to Kai's room and they start smoking but you don't want to be around smoke, what do you do? Well, boundaries are not about telling Kai they can't smoke in their own room. Remember, boundaries are the rules and limits that help you live in alignment with your values—in this case, the value of not wanting to be around cigarette smoke.

To support those values, the first step is letting other people know what they are. On a basic level, this is what boundary setting is: communicating your values and what you need to live in accordance with them. So you say to Kai, "Hey, I'm not comfortable being around smoke." Now that Kai knows what your values are (in contrast to hoping they'll intuit this by noticing you wrinkling your nose or saying something indirect like, "Wow, I can't believe you're still smoking"), they have an opportunity to respond. Perhaps they say, "Oh shoot, I really wanted to finish this cigarette. Would you mind if we went outside and kept talking?" Based on Kai's response, you get to choose (and communicate) whether you're okay with stepping outside or if you need something else.

But let's say Kai responds, um...a little *differently*. They say, "Screw you! I'm allowed to smoke in my room!" Well, they're right. I mean, they're also being a bit of a jerk, but they are correct: they are allowed to smoke in their own room. The key, though, is that boundaries allow for *both* of you to live in alignment with your values, even when those values differ. So you might say, "Okay, I'm going to step out while you finish your cigarette." You're not telling Kai what to do, but you are clarifying your own limits and rules.

This distinction is super important, because I have found, both in my own experience and listening to others, that when we confuse boundary setting with trying to control what someone else does, thinks, or feels, our task feels *way* harder than it actually is. If, in the above example, boundary setting required you to convince Kai that they should quit smoking, good luck! That's about a billion times more difficult than letting Kai know you're going to step out while they smoke. So focusing on what your limits and rules are is a fantastic way to make boundary setting easier for you and considerate of other people's agency.

Boundaries and the Witch's Circle

In my witchcraft practice, I often cast a circle before I do a ritual, spell, journey meditation, etc. I can certainly do those things without a circle, just like we can have relationships without clear boundaries, but let's explore why I might take this extra step. For me, a circle isn't about suggesting that this space here is more sacred or magical than that space over there; it's about clarifying what the space is being used for. If I'm doing a Full Moon ritual, I might cast a circle with the intention of connecting more deeply with the energy of the Moon. When I'm in the circle, I'm more focused on my aim because I've set aside the space specifically for that purpose.

Similarly, boundaries aren't about saying "my needs are better or more important than yours." They're about creating a space where I'm focused on living in alignment with my values, and you're allowed to do the same in your space. If I'm going to visit your space, your boundaries serve as clear guidelines for how I can behave respectfully in your space without having to guess, which can be a lot of work! Boundaries are a way of saying, "Hey, I respect your time and energy. I won't ask you to read my mind when I can clearly communicate what I need."

Another benefit to casting a magic circle is it facilitates connection with spirit guides and deities. We can absolutely connect with these beings without a circle, but just like when throwing a party, it's easier for everyone to show up if a clear time and place have been established. Inside the circle, this boundary helps everyone focus on the task at hand. For instance, if I'm calling my guides to a money-spellcasting circle, both my guides and I know when and where to show up and that we're here to do some money magic. And if my guides aren't in the mood for a money spell that day, this also gives them the opportunity to bow out, because I've been clear about my intent.

> **Boundaries aren't about saying "my needs are better or more important than yours." They're about creating a space where I'm focused on living in alignment with my values, and you're allowed to do the same in your space.**

Similarly, our personal boundaries facilitate connection to other people by letting them know how we'd like to connect, giving them the choice to participate or not based on their own needs. For example, if you're aware that my boundaries involve not staying up past 10:00 p.m., you'll know you have a much better chance of seeing me if you reach out before my bedtime. Boundaries are a way of communicating what matters to us (our values) and listening to what matters to others. Rather than assuming that we all value the same things, we can set boundaries to honor the fact that we're unique individuals. Boundaries communicate, "Hey, I'm interested in getting to know your uniqueness. I don't expect you to be just like me." What a profound gift to offer in our relationships! Far from being rude or unkind, healthy boundaries create space for all of us to be who we are and to connect from a place of authenticity.

Finally, casting a magic circle helps us connect not only with others but also with ourselves. I build a relationship with myself by getting clear on what I want and intentionally carving out time to focus on that pursuit, such as meditating or drawing tarot cards. This sends the message that my wants and needs are valued, and because I've set aside focused time instead of just hoping for the best amid the bustle of daily life, I'm more likely to hear my inner voice and connect with my intuition. As a result, my life feels more satisfying and purposeful, like something I am actively, creatively participating in as opposed to events that are merely happening *to* me.

Our personal boundaries do the same by helping us honor our own needs within the busyness and competing demands of the world. Without boundaries, life is all too happy to fill our schedules with tasks that might have very little to do with our genuine priorities, and we can end each day feeling exhausted yet wondering what we even accomplished. Being able to mark out time and space to tend to our needs keeps us connected to the quiet voice of our soul, without which we often feel aimless and despondent.

The comparison of drawing boundaries to circle casting isn't arbitrary. We can employ energetic tools like circles to help us set boundaries with other people. Before communicating a boundary, you might spend a few minutes focusing on the "magic circle" that is your aura, filling it with white light or a color that feels supportive to you, strengthening the outer surface with the intent that nothing harmful may enter, etc. Use your magical skills to support your boundary setting!

How to Set Boundaries

Learning to set boundaries involves (1) getting clear on what our boundaries are and (2) taking care of ourselves while we set them, because boundary setting, especially if we're new to it, can feel downright scary! Getting clear on your boundaries is often as simple as taking some time to shift your attention inward. When we're drowning in other people's expectations and the chatter of life, it's easy to lose touch with our inner knowing, but our needs are often very present, just below the surface.

For me, journaling is a great way to flesh out what I need, and a surefire way to identify a boundary is to journal about something in your life that triggers resentment. Let yourself freewrite about the situation, and pay attention to descriptions of what you think other people should or shouldn't be doing, for instance, "My mom shouldn't tell me what to do with my life! I'm forty years old!" or "How dare Bryce leave his report for me to do. That's his job!" These are clear indicators that your values aren't being honored, which is a perfect place to practice boundary setting.

Let's take the example of the advice-giving mom to illustrate how to translate this inner awareness into clearly communicated boundaries. After journaling, you realize that whenever your mom shares what she thinks you should do in your dating life, you feel like crap. This is great to know! You're now clear that you value being able to chart your own course in dating, and boundaries will help you live in alignment with that value. Here are some ways to communicate this boundary. Next time your mom starts to offer unsolicited advice, you could say, "Mom, I appreciate how much you care, but I need to make my own choices here. I'm not looking for dating advice." If she continues, you could say, "Mom, I'm not open to hearing dating advice. I'd like to talk about something else."

It can feel challenging if the other person isn't skilled when it comes to honoring boundaries and they try to argue with you. The first thing to note is that this is their issue. It's not your responsibility to make people understand or agree with your boundaries. Your job is simply to do your best to clearly communicate what your boundaries are. If you grew up in a wounded family system like I did, this might feel totally against the rules! "Wait, what? I don't have to take responsibility for other people's feelings and needs?" Nope. In these scenarios, you might sound like a broken record, restating your boundary multiple times, and that's okay. You don't need to launch into lengthy explanations, defenses, or apologies, because this is rarely an issue of the person not understanding but rather is usually about them not wanting to respect your boundary.

> **You might sound like a broken record, restating your boundary multiple times….You don't need to launch into lengthy explanations, defenses, or apologies, because this is rarely an issue of the person not understanding but rather is usually about them not wanting to respect your boundary.**

And guess what? You're also allowed to set boundaries around how many times you repeat a boundary! For instance, if you've made it clear that you don't want your mom's dating advice, and you've restated the boundary but she's *still* not respecting it, you have the right to end the conversation: "Mom, I've said I'm not open to dating advice. I'm going to let you go and we can talk another time."

This brings us to the second piece of boundary setting: taking care of ourselves while we set them. It's possible that just reading those hypothetical exchanges has your heart pounding and your armpits sweating. I feel you! Boundary setting can feel super awkward or like we're doing something "bad," particularly if we were raised in wounded family systems that didn't model or permit healthy boundaries. Therapy is one of my favorite supports for processing intense thoughts and feelings and learning new boundary-setting skills.

Finally, know that you can set boundaries even when you feel uncomfortable. In fact, even after you gain more practice setting boundaries, it's likely that you'll still encounter guilt or awkwardness at times. That's okay. You're not doing it wrong if you feel those things—you're just human! You care about being kind and you don't want to hurt people's feelings, and you can honor both of those intentions *while* setting boundaries. Remember, boundaries aren't attacking or rude; they're simply the limits and rules that help you—and others—live in accordance with your values, and that's a beautiful thing.

Melissa Tipton *is a Jungian Witch, Structural Integrator, and founder of the Real Magic Mystery School, where she teaches online courses in Jungian Magic, a potent blend of ancient magical techniques and modern psychological insights. She's the author of* Living Reiki: Heal Yourself and Transform Your Life *and* Llewellyn's Complete Book of Reiki. *Learn more and take a free class at www.realmagic.school.*

Illustrator: M. Kathryn Thompson

Untangling Magical Misfires

Cerridwen Iris Shea

It happens. There's exploding desire, strength of will, the tools. There's even the research and the divination on the spell. The spell is performed. It lands. It manifests.

But it turns out to be the wrong choice.

We've all had those magical misfires. Some of them are comic. Some break our hearts. But how do we untangle ourselves from them?

It's not easy. It's not painless. But it's possible.

Early in training or explorations, it's likely the misfire had to do with a love spell. Casting a love spell on a specific individual can backfire because after six months you realize this should have been a short-term relationship and this isn't the person with whom you want to stay. Now you've tied that person to you and need to do a spell or sequence of spells to loosen the ties with harmony. Another situation is where you discover you have to renew the love spell at shorter and shorter intervals, and it takes more and more energy. Sometimes the individual on whom the spell is cast turns into a stalker; other times the consequence may be that the spell triggers intense dislike.

One of the reasons love spells on specific individuals are discouraged is that you can't make someone love you; you have to let them love you. Don't interfere with their free will or bodily autonomy. Another reason is that this individual may be attractive to you now, but they might not be the right person for the kind of long-term, healthy, loving partnership you want. Tying this individual to you pushes away the better relationship.

Misfires can happen by accident. In a moment of anger, we throw out an impulsive thought with a force of will behind it, and we later learn it manifested in a way that caused pain or chaos that we did not intend. We regret sending it, or we discover that the anger was directed at the

One of the reasons love spells on specific individuals are discouraged is that you can't make someone love you; you have to let them love you. Don't interfere with their free will or bodily autonomy.

wrong party. If you believe someone is working against you and give to them what you believe you're getting from them, only to find out that the person who told you about this other individual was lying or there was a miscommunication, it will be a mess. That's one reason a spell that returns the energy to the sender or (my preference) a spell that transforms negative energy into positive is often a stronger choice.

There are times when you do the research, work out the possible consequences, believe it's the right choice, then do a strong spell or series of spells, and it still doesn't work in your best interest. Maybe you didn't have all the information. Maybe you realized that the spell's original goal and what you actually need are different. But you still need to find a way out.

There are many paths in the Craft. Wicca has the "rule of three," where what you put out comes back to you threefold. The rule of three does not apply only to repercussions for the caster (although it's often used that way). It's meant to make the caster think about the potential long-term ramifications. By thinking it through and considering the various possibilities and consequences, you can hone the spell and make it as specific as possible so it doesn't have a detrimental effect, or as few detrimental effects as possible.

There are also paths where the practitioners believe there's no point in having the power to create change, be it positive or negative, unless one uses it. They have their own tenets and their own beliefs in potential consequences.

There's not a single way to make a spell. There's not a single way to break a spell.

And if it was a sequenced spell that you cast, it may take an enormous amount of time and energy and another sequence of spells to undo it.

Sequenced Spells

What do I mean by "sequenced" spells? When I do a series of rituals and/or spells over time to reinforce or build onto my goal, or if a series of spells done close together is needed to handle multiple facets of a goal, that's what I call a sequenced spell. Reinforcing the protections/wards monthly around my home is just that—reinforcing. But if I perform a set of spells with different purposes to achieve a specific goal, that is a sequenced spell.

I once did a spell to manifest what I believed was my dream job. I interviewed and wanted the job more than anything. I did several spells over a series of weeks to manifest this particular job (instead of "the best job for me at this time"). I got the job. Four days after I was hired, my boss left. Her replacement was devious, vicious, jealous, insecure, and determined to break me. She didn't break me, but she did some damage. She eventually fired me, which was the best possible outcome, and it took a lot of work for me to realize what had happened and how to heal from it.

My biggest magical misfire was when I moved to the ocean after decades of living in a city. I had dreamed of living in this location since I was six years old. I talked about "someday" moving there. When I was in my late forties, I did. I was convinced I would spend the rest of my life there. Even though I was in a rented house (which I loved), I did rooting spells to stay (spells that helped me "put down roots" in my new location). The reality was that this was not my forever home. While I had a strong connection to the land, I never found the community or the opportunities as a resident that I'd had as a visiting artist. I had dreamed of a community that was there in the 1920s or the 1960s or maybe had never existed there at all except in fantasy. My path lay elsewhere.

I got signs, but ignored them, and kept rooting. During the first year of the pandemic, I fought two kinds of cancer, making "the rest of my life there" nearly a reality, but not in the way I wanted. During the second year of the pandemic, my landlord decided to sell the house, and I was forced to move. The move, which "uprooted" forcefully all the work I'd done, was brutal on me, physically, emotionally, and spiritually. I was lucky to land in an amazing place in the mountains that offered much of what I'd dreamed the place at the sea would offer (except for the sea itself). It took nearly a year after the move to undo that magical misfire, and I haven't done any rooting spells in the new location, as much as I love it.

What Went Wrong and Why

When something goes cattywampus in a spell, sit down and figure out why. This is a time to be brutally honest with yourself and face any unpleasant truths about why you made the choices you did. Look for signs you missed or ignored, and figure out what went wrong. This takes time, and it might not be pleasant, but it's necessary. Write about it in your personal or magical journal. Do a series of tarot readings. In one spread ask, "What went wrong?" In the second spread ask, "What signs did I miss that warned me?" In the third spread ask, "What actions can I take to heal and move forward?" You can use a traditional Celtic Cross spread for each question, or you can mix and match spreads.

> **When something goes cattywampus in a spell, sit down and figure out why. This is a time to be brutally honest with yourself and face any unpleasant truths about why you made the choices you did.**

Once you know what went wrong and have ideas on how to fix it, you can start with some spells to undo what went wrong and then build new spells to create something better. Here are some options.

Cut the Cord Spell

If you did a cord spell as a catalyst to this misfire, you can do a similar spell as a step to undo it. Most cord spells have you make nine knots in a cord of a specific color. As the spell manifests, you undo the knots one by one and then burn the cord (or do a spell to neutralize the cord, if it's a cord you use over and over).

For this spell you need:

• A length of black cord, about a yard long

• A pair of scissors

• A fireproof dish and some matches or a lighter

• Pen and paper

Make a list of nine mistakes in connection with your misfired spell, and a step to transform each one into a positive.

Tie nine knots in the cord. Starting at one end, speak each mistake as you knot: "I was wrong about (fill in mistake)." Leave space between each knot. A thirty-six-inch cord will have knots about every four inches. You need to leave an inch or so at each end. Do not tie the knots tightly, because you will be undoing them.

Hold the knotted cord in your hand. Accept that the initial spell was not the best choice, and now you are taking action to fix it.

Cut off the first knot, leaving enough space between cuts to make untying easy. Hold the knot and say, "I release this mistake by (add in the action to fix it)." Untie the knot, then set it on fire and burn it in the fireproof dish. Do this with each knot.

When the cord is completely burned, wait until it cools and dispose of the burnt cord away from your property. Return home, take a ritual bath, and begin the nine steps to fix the mistake.

Separation Spell

There are versions of this spell in many different spell books and traditions. This is the variation I use to separate from a person, job, or situation. I use candles in the shape of what I want to separate (such as figure candles if I want to separate from a person) or just plain tapers. Black candles work the fastest for me; white ones work slowly and more gently. If I want to give the spell an additional boost, I have a single magenta candle burning beside the spell while it's going (and extinguish it when I extinguish the others).

This spell centers on getting me out of a situation. The purpose is not to separate someone from their partner because I want one of them. In my belief system, that would be interfering with free will, and I don't do it.

You will need:

- 2 tall taper candles in sturdy holders

- A knife or carving tool for the candles

- Uncrossing oil, rosemary oil, or clary sage oil

- A nine-inch length of black ribbon

- Scissors

Carve your name into one candle. Carve the name of who or what you wish to separate from into the second candle. Mark eight equal lines on each candle. (These lines will indicate how far down you burn the candles during each session, with the last "line" being the bottom of each candle.) Anoint both candles with oil and secure them in holders.

Tie the black ribbon onto the bottom of each candle secured in its holder or to the bottom of each holder. Place them together so the ribbon hangs loose and the candleholders touch.

Light the candles and say, "We separate in love, harmony, peace, and goodwill."

When the candles burn down to the first line, extinguish them, saying, "The flame rests; the energy continues." (Do not blow them out. Use a snuffer or your fingers.)

The next day, move the candles a little farther apart. Relight them and speak the lighting incantation. Extinguish with the extinguishing incantation. Burn down the candles each day to the next line, moving the holders farther apart each time.

On the ninth and final day, the ribbon should be taut between the candles. Light the candles with the incantation. Now cut the cord with the scissors, saying, "We are free of each other and continue on our separate paths in love, harmony, and goodwill." You can move the candles farther apart or even into separate rooms to burn out. Remove the cut ribbons and dispose of them the next time you leave the premises. Let the candles burn all the way out.

This spell works best on a waning moon. If you time it to end on the dark moon, even better. It can be done whenever there is a strong need. If you need to do it all at once, the waning moon is strongest, but it can be done as needed. If you do it in one session, move the candles farther apart as they burn down to each line, then separate them near the end.

Do not leave the burning candles unattended. I use glass hurricane holders or tubes even if I'm in the same room (because I have curious cats).

Dissolving Spell

I burn spell components to release manifestation energy, so when I want to "unmanifest" something, I prefer to dissolve it. I've used this spell when dealing with insurance or social service agencies or customer service situations where the act of contacting them manifests the obstacle and "dissolving" it smooths the path to the solution. I've also used it to dissolve a creative partnership that wasn't working for either of us but the other party did not want to let go out of ego or fear.

I burn spell components to release manifestation energy, so when I want to "unmanifest" something, I prefer to dissolve it.

You will need:

• A sugar cube OR a small piece of paper and water-soluble ink

• A bowl of consecrated water

If you are using pen and ink, write down what you want to untangle. If you are using a sugar cube, hold it gently (so it doesn't crumble) in your hand and imagine the obstacle inhabiting the cube.

Drop the sugar cube or the inked paper into the bowl and swirl it around, saying, "Power of water, dissolve this manifestation, healing all pain and discord it caused. Dissipate the energy, to be gathered in the future for something beautiful. So mote it be."

Watch the sugar or paper dissolve. See if any of the shapes it takes as it dissipates has meaning. If you used paper, remove the paper and throw it out away from your property. If you used sugar, pour the water/sugar water down the drain and follow it with vinegar. As it washes down the drain, imagine it going through the pipes and away from you.

Untangling Spell

This spell is useful for muddled communications where people talk past each other instead of with each other, and every exchange grows more fraught. You need a hunk of tangled yarn. (Yarn is easier to work with than thread.) Sit with the yarn, working through the tangles and thinking through how and where poor choices were made, how to adjust them, and what you've learned from them. When the yarn is untangled, roll it up into a neat ball or skein, imagining how you will create something better.

Energy Dance Transformation Spell

This spell works when you feel negative energy coming at you. Sit quietly. Call or pull up energy from the ground and air around you, visualizing it in bright, shimmering colors, taking the form of dancers. Then imagine the negative energy taking the shape of dancers but in dark colors. Have the energy dancers meet, touch, and dance together. (You can play music. You can join in the dance.) Let the dancers whirl around, faster and faster. The negative energy taps into and is affected by the joy of the dance. It turns brighter and transforms into positive energy. (The colors might still be dark, but they won't be dull; they'll grow brighter.) Once the energy is transformed, shake out your hands. See all the dancers turn into iridescent particles of energy and dissipate. Place your palms on the floor to ground and center.

Healing and Acceptance

We are human. We make mistakes. We make poor decisions. We pay the price. We atone, make amends, and work to make it right.

During this process, it's often difficult to forgive ourselves for the mistakes we've made. But forgiveness is a vital part of the process to accept, heal, and make things right.

I find that working with crystals in deep meditation sessions, at least twice a day, helps the healing, along with intensive journal writing sessions. As a Pisces, my birthstones of aquamarine and bloodstone give any work I do a boost. For healing and acceptance, I work with pink opal and/or labradorite. I also find lemon topaz to be a general energy and mood enhancer. Working with citrus oils (especially tangerine) helps too.

I sit twice a day, for at least ten minutes at a time, holding the stones and working on accepting that I'm a flawed human who makes mistakes, learns from them, and tries to do better moving forward. This is a separate, additional practice from my daily meditation sessions, and I make time for it. I also dive deep as I write in my journal, no matter how painful or uncomfortable it gets. Discomfort is part of the learning and healing process.

If the original spell that went awry was a sequenced spell, chances are a sequenced spell is needed to rectify it. But the first step is to identify where it went wrong and why, in order to build the spell or spells needed to realign the energies. For instance, I would choose either the cut the cord, separation, or untangling spell and perform that. Then I would do a dissolving spell, followed by the energy dance, followed by the healing and acceptance.

Making It Right and Moving Forward

Once you've done the untangling work, consider whether you need to make amends to someone. Do you owe anyone an apology or a note of thanks? Do you need to take action to fix the pain you caused? If you've done a spell to break a connection, sometimes it is best not to have further contact. In some situations, doing something kind or helpful but doing so anonymously is the best choice. Other times you may offer an apology but it is not accepted; the other party has the right to make that choice. Ponder your own situation and make the strongest, most positive choices for all involved that you can.

We all struggle. We're all doing the best we can. Sometimes our plan doesn't work. Sometimes we cause unintentional harm. But we can work to make it right, learn from it, and work on doing better.

Cerridwen Iris Shea *was an urban witch, then a sea witch, and is now a mountain witch, and always a kitchen witch and tarot reader. She is a full-time writer, publishing under multiple names in fiction and nonfiction, and is an internationally produced playwright and radio writer. Visit her website at www.cerridwenscottage.com.*

Illustrator: Bri Hermanson

Timing Your Spells
for Maximum Magic
Madame Pamita

Probably one of the most empowering parts of being a witch is spellcasting. Can you still be a witch and not
cast spells? Of course. But why miss out
on all that fun? I love to cast spells and
see the amazing results that they bring,
and you probably do too. Every time we
cast a spell, it reminds us that even in a
culture that is constantly attempting
to exert power over us, we have agency
over ourselves. A spell is a statement: as
witches, we have the final say in making
our lives the beautiful adventures they
were meant to be.

When I shifted from working in a coven to being a solitary witch, I thought that whenever I was casting a spell, I had to raise all the power by myself and keep that energy going to make my spell fly. Then I had the insight that even as a solitary, you are never doing your spells on your own. Whenever you make magic, you are inviting in spirits, deities, herbs, crystals, words, elements, magical tools, and many other spiritual allies to work with you. These allies are there to focus your intention. They help keep the energy of the spell moving forward whenever you might waver. When we invite this support system in, we have to do less of the heavy lifting to get to our manifestations.

Even as a solitary, you are never doing your spells on your own. Whenever you make magic, you are inviting in spirits, deities, herbs, crystals, words, elements, magical tools, and many other spiritual allies to work with you.

When we think of these allies, we often think of the spirits and objects that we bring to our craft, but there is another aspect of our craft that can help make our spells take off: the time when we do our magic. The timing of spells can bring a mindfulness and energetic support to our intentions. Casting a spell is like pushing a wheelbarrow. You *can* push a wheelbarrow uphill, but when we optimize the timing of our spell, it can make our magic flow, like pushing the wheelbarrow down a gentle slope. If you don't want to have to do your spell over and over again to get the desired result, maybe it's time to incorporate some timing into your magic.

There are those emergency situations where we may not have the luxury of time, and if that's the case, then do your spell right away. But if you have the opportunity to enhance your spell with a special timing, there are a lot of ways you can bring in that power.

Seasonal Timings

The seasons have a strong influence on spellwork. People going back to prehistoric times paid attention to the ebb and flow of the light and dark, the changes in weather, and the effect that it had on the natural world around them. These powers can be optimized for your magic. Springtime energy can be harnessed for fertility and new beginnings, summer for gathering of forces, autumn for harvesting our accomplishments, and winter for regrouping, resting, and planning.

Wiccans, pagans and traditional folk magic practitioners can see the energies of these seasonal events in the sabbats of the Wheel of the Year and in pagan holiday traditions. You can reverse engineer your magic by paying attention to these special celebrations and designing spells that coincide with the energy of the season.

Astrological Timings

For witches interested in the influence of the planets, you can optimize your spells by choosing an auspicious astrological timing. Those who are knowledgeable about electional astrology can choose the best time to start their spellwork by creating a chart, but even witches with a basic understanding of the signs of the zodiac can use planetary positions to their advantage.

The sun moves through the twelve signs throughout each calendar year. Each of these zodiac signs has certain characteristics, and doing your spell during that sun sign can reinforce the particular energy of your spell. For example, if you were doing a spell for more popularity or leadership, you could start it during Leo season to amplify that power.

Can't wait for the sun to get to your desired sign? The moon moves through each sign about every two and a half days and goes through the entire zodiac in a month, so you have lots of chances to create an optimal timing. Check out a moon calendar or app to discern when the moon will hit your astrological sweet spot.

Moon Timings

In addition to astrological signs, the moon also moves through phases as it appears to change throughout the month. This growing and shrinking of the lit portion of the moon is called waxing and waning. The waxing moon is when the moon appears to be getting larger in the sky night by night—moving from the first tiny sliver all the way up to the full moon. The waning moon is when the moon appears to be getting smaller—going from full moon back down to a thin crescent and then the new moon.

The waxing moon is perfect for spells where your intention is to attract, increase, start, or grow. The waning moon phase is ideal for magic that includes banishing, diminishing, stopping, or decreasing. The waxing and waning phases each take about two weeks, so there is plenty of time to do spells over multiple days and harness the increasing or decreasing energy.

Don't forget the very special times of the full moon and new moon as support for your spellwork. The full moon is perfect for communal spells done with others for group intentions, while the new moon or dark moon is the best time to do solitary personal work.

Day of the Week Timings

The days of the week also have their particular energies and can be used for timing our spells as well. Each of the days is aligned with a planet and its corresponding goddess or god from the Germanic or Greek pantheon. Select a day of the week that most closely matches the intent of your spell, or do a different type of magic each day of the week.

Sunday corresponds to the Sun and is perfect for spells of leadership, healing, blessing, success, and popularity.

Monday is the Moon day and is great for mystical magic such as working with spirits, developing psychic ability, dreamwork, and personal emotional spells for self-love, family, home, and children.

Tuesday is named after Tiw/Tyr and corresponds to the planet Mars. Cast a spell on Tuesday for strength, courage, and vitality, as well as victory in competitive situations or outright battle.

Wednesday is named after Woden/Odin and is attached to the planet Mercury. Wednesday is a great day to do spells for communication, travel, gambling luck, or transactional business.

Thursday is Thor's day and the day of the planet Jupiter. Cast a spell on Thursday for prosperity, expansion, power, business growth, attracting clients, and legal matters.

Friday is named after the goddess Freya and corresponds to the planet Venus. Friday is ideal for spells related to love, beauty, harmony, creativity, pleasure, and attraction magic.

Saturday is named after the god and planet Saturn and can be used for magic of restriction, binding, or limitation, as well as spells for motivation, will, and knowledge.

Time of Day Timings

Like our most ancient ancestors, we can tap into special times of day that have an empowering effect on our intentions. Get outside and observe the daylight or dark and use it to charge up your magic.

Sunrise can be utilized for new beginnings, fresh starts, increase, and growth. Noon, or when the sun is at its apex in the sky, can be used for spells of success, strength, power, abundance, and material wealth. Sunset is ideal for spells of releasing, cleansing, banishing, or endings. Midnight, or halfway between dusk and dawn, is called the "witching hour" for a reason—it's the most powerful time to do spells for spirit contact, psychic work, or working in other spiritual realms.

For witches who are attuned to numerology, it's also possible to time your spell by the hours on the clock. Choose a time and number that corresponds to your intent. For example, in numerology, the number 2 corresponds to partnerships and so can be used for romantic spells as well as successful business or friendship spells. Starting your spell at 2:02 or 2:22 can amplify this harmonious energy.

Combining Spell Timings

Bringing any one of these timings into your magic can augment the intention of your spellwork and bring more success, but if you feel ambitious, you can combine these spell timing methods to add even more support for your spell. For example, you could start your spell on a Friday during the waxing moon phase to attract a new love, or you could do a banishing spell at sunset when the moon is in Scorpio.

Think of all the creative ways you can incorporate timings into your magic and bring even more juiciness to your spells. Remember, you don't have to do all the heavy lifting yourself. As a witch, time is on your side.

Madame Pamita *is a Ukrainian diaspora witch, teacher, author, candlemaker, spellcaster, and tarot reader. She has a popular* YouTube *channel for teaching witchcraft, she hosts the* Magic and the Law of Attraction *and* Baba Yaga's Magic *podcasts, and she is the author of* Baba Yaga's Book of Witchcraft, The Book of Candle Magic, *and* Madame Pamita's Magical Tarot. *She is also the proprietress of the Parlour of Wonders, an online spiritual apothecary, and lives in Santa Monica, California. You can find her at parlourofwonders.com.*

Illustrator: Tim Foley

Disposal and Cleansing
of Magickal Items

Diana Rajchel

The video, sent to me by a friend, displayed something I see much too often: a man with a giant magnet fishing strange objects out of a river. As I watched and cringed, he sifted through the contents of his catch: three nesting cauldrons containing a few horseshoes, a railroad spike, some plant matter, and a long chain.

I am the person people call when someone opens that box that's probably haunted or retrieves that weird object floating down the river, and as a result of that choice ends up with weird nightmares involving caterpillars or unable to find their car keys for the next year. Here is what I have to say to those people: if you got it out, don't put it back. You let the spirit out of the bottle, and closing the door or casting it back into the water isn't the thing that needs to be done now. Follow along; I'll tell you what to do with it.

Most people reading this are on the other end of the "found ritual objects" situation. We need to be aware that we live in a world where not only will people find our ritual detritus but they'll also post it on the Internet. It's time to reevaluate our disposal methods and change some of them.

When you practice magick, especially folk forms that use physical tools, even the sturdiest of tools will reach the end of their life span at some point. We expect short-term use of incense and candles, but sometimes jewelry and cauldrons also reach a breaking point, and when that happens, they deserve a place to break down in peace.

We also often need disposal as part of keeping our home energy clean, and many practices use removing spell components as a signal to spirit that a spell has finished. Folk magick follows thermodynamics in its design, and that means most spells must allow room for entropy.

Entropy is a natural process of degradation in the universal cycle of energy. As a spell becomes less relevant or goes unmaintained, the energy within it—all those intentions, shapes, directions, and elements—breaks down. While rotting magick usually doesn't smell bad, you might end up experiencing the feeling of rot. And like decay in the physical world, the breakdown of the original energy can draw the attention of entities that, for most people, emit a most discomforting sensation. The best way to prevent this discomfort is to clean up after ourselves and to remove old spell components from our environment.

OG Ritual Item Disposal

In original-edition magickal item disposal, most items moved on in one of three ways: burial, burning, or drowning. Burial returns what emerged from the earth to its natural decay process and grounds out any kickback from the spell. Burning, whether herb or candle, produces a transformation, and on a physical level hopefully leaves only ash behind. If a little wax remains at the end of a candle burn, the wax can be melted for a new candle or buried. Drowning—usually by tossing an item into running water—carries the bad energy or person away, and at some point the life in the river consumes the life connected to the spell.

Sometimes, if the spell components are biodegradable or reusable, we can still use the bury, burn, drown approach. But as in all practices, magickal practitioners have room for improvement—especially as we learn from one another about what works for us and what sometimes works against us.

Updated Disposal Methods

If you make it a point to use only biodegradable materials that break down fast for your spells, you may not need to change much. These new approaches I'm advocating for came about because of my own mistakes. For instance, if you use nylon threads in a charm bag or poppet, the spell may not deactivate naturally. This leads to a weird situation of ever-fresh stagnation. Throwing items in water can pollute community resources, lead to angry visits from spirits of that element, and be discovered by fishers or people attempting water cleanup. Fire is always a risk.

Over the years, when I needed to move, I had to get creative with old spell materials. Sometimes relocation necessitated the change in approach, and other times limitations on privacy were the primary factor. The following methods have all worked well for me.

Cleanse and Reuse

Resetting, cleansing, and reusing magickal items isn't a new process, but it often ends up left out of the "for best results" directions. Practitioners maintain a lot of standard methods, like smoke cleansing with prairie sage or spritzing with salt water, because they are generally effective. However, the standbys aren't the best in every situation, and methods that will work in their place aren't always intuitive.

For example, if you use nightmare traps, you need not throw one away or burn it when it appears to stop working. Most traps of this nature reset after you leave them in direct sunlight for about four hours. From there, you can spruce them up with a spray that attracts interfering energies to the trap and away from you. Here is a recipe you can use for this.

Attract the Astral Critters Cleansing Spray

Make a tea from the following plants for this spray (but do not ingest this!):

- 1 tablespoon catnip
- 1 tablespoon poppy petals (any species)
- 1 tablespoon mushrooms (any type available at your grocery store)
- A tiny chunk of dragon's blood resin
- A splash of crème de violette liqueur

Bring to a simmer. Maintain at the same temperature for seven minutes, then allow to cool.

Strain through a coffee filter and pour into a spray bottle. Spritz your nightmare or spirit traps with this spray just after they are done sunbathing.

Forever Items

Certain ritual tools—athames, bolines, mirrors, and other permanent items—require regular cleansing. (Every six weeks or right before each sabbat is reasonable.) Waving them through a cedar or rosemary incense usually does the job. However, when these tools break or when someone dies, they sometimes need a different approach.

Jewelry especially can have a strong personal connection to prior keepers. Many such items can be gently reset by waving a selenite wand over them on all sides. However, some pieces can retain magickal programming despite that. If you don't know fully what the original intention was, you can't know for sure what a previous person programmed the item to do. If you don't have all the information about any intentions embedded in it, you may not be able to prevent unintended results. In situations where you just don't have enough information, and for whatever reason you don't have the means for mediumship or divination, your best bet is to remove all previous energetic programming from the item.

> **Jewelry especially can have a strong personal connection to prior keepers.... In situations where you just don't have enough information,...your best bet is to remove all previous energetic programming from the item.**

You can do this with baker's ammonia, or if you want to avoid using a harsh chemical or have an allergy, hematite combined with Hawaiian black salt can do the same, albeit more slowly.

To clear the energy on an item with baker's ammonia, dip a paint-brush in the powder and swipe it on the object. The effect is close to instant. If you use hematite and salt, then place the item in a bowl of said material and leave it where it can sit undisturbed for a day and a night.

I'm Done, but I Don't Want to Throw It Out. Now What?

Witches see ritual items as highly personal, and in the US we have built a culture around never sharing or getting rid of our most precious items. The practice has shifted in these growing days of "waste not, want not." Some items we connect to less than others, and rather than throw them away, we may attempt to find them new homes. More people are participating in tarot card swaps or selling old witchcraft tools on eBay and elsewhere as their practices evolve and change, and that calls for a shift in our magickal hygiene practices.

If you decide you want to pass your tools on, perform a cut-and-clear working to sever your energy from the tool you used. This helps the next person make the item much more their own and relieves you of any accidental energy burden through a remaining connection. To do this working, tie a natural-fiber string between the object and yourself, feel that connection to the tool, and then cut that cord. When finished, go ahead and burn or throw away the cord. Unless the item is spirit-inhabited, that should be all you need to end that connection.

Special Care Disposables

Folk magick has certain spells with physical items that you can't just give away, and using the burn, bury, drown method may have undesired results. Examples of this are poppets and charm bags. Most poppets are made with an intentional likeness and connection to another human being. Before you "switch off" the magick, perform a cut-and-clear between the poppet and the person it represents. Without that energy severance, the magick won't clear fully from the likeness. Again, you need some biodegradable string (such as cotton or hemp) and scissors. Tie one string to the poppet and hold the other string in your hand. State your intention to sever the connection between the representation of the person and the actual person. After the cut, the poppet will retain some energy. Give the poppet a quick swipe of ammonia powder, which should hit its energetic off switch. You can also use the previous hematite and salt method in this scenario.

Most poppets are made with an intentional likeness and connection to another human being. Before you "switch off" the magick, perform a cut-and-clear between the poppet and the person it represents.

After you have severed ties and drained the magickal energy, you can disassemble the poppet and sort out the ingredients for composting or reuse. In the case of items such as dream pillows and charm bags, you don't need to sever ties—you can just jump straight to the magickal off switch.

Disposing of Inhabited Items

While rare, it's not unheard of for a spirit to reside inside a magickal object. Usually, either the spirit was deliberately trapped in a crystal—and often sent there for a good reason—or it decided it wanted to live in that resin skull you picked up at Target for Halloween one year. Spirits, like any other being, have minds of their own and often need a place to rest. Whether you need them to leave or you want them living in your Halloween skulls is between you and your gods.

If you don't want a spirit living in whatever item it has nested in, the ammonia off switch won't work. It may even cause the spirit to become grumpy with you. If you want the spirit gone, you usually need its buy-in.

To handle a spirit-inhabited object that you don't want to keep, you have a few options:

1. Obtain some permanent and remote storage for the spirit-inhabited object. If it's bad news, you might encase the object in cement, rent a security deposit box that you are confident will continue to be paid for forever that it can live in, or inveigle it into a time capsule (which is probably the worst choice, as you are then making it someone else's problem).

2. You can talk to the spirit and give it somewhere else to go. I often suggest that the spirit go to the ocean for rebirth or return to its place of origin. If none of those options sound good, I suggest that the spirit disperse itself into the elements or the stars.

3. If, for some reason, the spirit wants to hang out but you need the item containing it, you can use a method known to those in any culture that has ever grown squash: give the spirit a gourd to live in. Unless you know how to dry gourds and the exact right types to use for containers, purchase the gourd from a local crafter. You can paint it with sigils, and if you don't mind the spirit existing near you, you could hang it on a nearby tree so it looks like a decoration to your neighbors.

New Methods for Cleansing and Clearing Magickal Objects

Because the way we live is changing—meaning that buried items no longer stay buried, and items given to water may not stay wet— we witches need a few extra ways to dispose of or cleanse our ritual items. You may want to use these new approaches, depending on the situation with the specific spell or ritual remains.

REWRITING THE ENERGY OF AN OBJECT

Rather than completely deconstruct a charm, you can rewrite the energy. A simple way to do this is to create a smoke bundle of herbs wrapped in brown paper filled with juniper berry, chaparral, and a pinch of myrrh. Then, while passing the item through the smoke, speak about how you need the item to shift its intent or manifestation. The process takes a few minutes. The more you talk about why you are shifting the intention and how you will know you have been successful, the more thorough the energy rewrite will be.

FORGING A NEW AGREEMENT WITH AN OBJECT

New agreements work best for animistic practitioners. To do this, talk to your ritual item and discuss how you want to work together. You may receive intuitions about what the item might need you to do, which is usually cleansing with something specific, such as cedar, or exposure to certain elements, like rain. So long as you follow through on that agreement, the sentient item can shift its expression.

FORWARDING THE ENERGY OF AN OBJECT

When practitioners talk about grounding the energy out of an object, they often mean that the energy from an item is absorbed by the planet itself. Grounding described this way is more accurately called *draining.* You can take another approach: redistribute the object's charged/added energy (as opposed to its innate energy) by dispersing it to the elements, going in all directions rather than just down. For example, setting an old watch next to a glass-encased candle and instructing the candle to take the magickal energy from it and disperse it to the elements of air and fire as it burns is a way of clearing the object without needing to destroy it. Dipping an item in running water (and pulling it back out) is another way to redistribute an energetic charge/magickal program in an object.

The Takeaways

A modern reality of magickal practice is that we have a world with less privacy than ever. When we literally send our ritual tools down a river, there is a reasonable chance of someone finding it, and its discovery may well end up on the Internet. Water everywhere is in a state of crisis, and the sewers themselves are starting to slap back with weird hauntings because of physical and metaphysical energy overload. While taking care to work only with ritual items that can decay and become obsolete or with energy sans tools (something that doesn't work for everyone) can offset some of this, physical spell and ritual tools touch something on a deep emotional level that the world still needs. We need ways to keep or safely pass on our ritual tools, or, if we must dispose of them, to ensure that they go undiscovered. The above methods, classic and new, all have an important place in continued practice, no matter where you fall on the spectrum of tradition. Shifting our cleansing and disposal practices of magickal items will go a long way toward keeping our spells secret, our magick undisturbed, and old men with big magnets from having weird things happening to them that they might not deserve.

Diana Rajchel *left her heart in San Francisco but moved most of her stuff to southwestern Michigan at the behest of her partner and dog. She is the author of such titles as* Urban Magick: A Guide for the City Witch *and* Hex Twisting: Countermagick Spells for the Irritated Witch. *She has begun the slow process of turning her home into an urban farm.*

https://www.dianarajchel.com
Instagram: drajchel
Facebook: dianarajchelauthor
Twitter: diana_rajchel
TikTok SpoonCherry01

Illustrator: M. Kathryn Thompson

Animism in the Elements

Kate Freuler

Like many witchy people, I feel that everything around me is alive. I don't mean just the obvious things like plants and animals, but also the soil, clouds, storms, and even places. Sometimes it's like they have personalities much like people. For example, a weeping willow tree hunched over a bog might seem to contain a wise old being, while a little pine sapling has a spritely, cute vibe to it.

My most profound experience with this phenomenon happened a few years ago. I was standing on a narrow peninsula

that stretched out into a huge bay. At my feet were bleached wood and broken shells that had been tossed out of the water like the skeletal remains of a meal. Despite the sunshine and calm, rippling waves, there was a distinctly ominous feel to the water. I can only describe it as hungry and merciless. I later found out that the placement of this peninsula creates deadly cross-currents, or undertows, deep beneath the calm surface and that many people had drowned there. Deceived by its gentle, welcoming appearance, people were seduced into the water only to be sucked under.

I know that to some this might just sound like my imagination got the best of me, but those with a natural understanding of animism know exactly what I mean when I say I could feel the living spirit in that part of the bay.

What Is Animism?

In a nutshell, animism is the belief that all things, including non-living things, possess a soul or spirit. This concept is easy to understand when applied to animals, especially pets, because they are individual beings with clear character traits. But when it comes to places and stationary objects, the idea of animism gets a little more abstract. Does a rock have a soul? Can a building be alive? Well, in my opinion, yes.

There are different ways to look at animism. On one level, it could be said that everything is composed of universal energy or life force. Some people believe this energy to be synonymous with soul or spirit, which would mean that everything is made of the same cosmic stuff as we are. In that way, everything contains a spirit. To take it further is the belief that in addition to all things being unified in this way, there are more refined, or individual, spirits within each thing as well. After all, not all dogs have the same personality and not all bodies of water are identical.

Discovering animism can enhance your experiences in all you encounter, touch, see, and interact with. What was once ordinary can become sacred, and when your life is full of sacredness, something revelatory and wonderful happens within you.

The Four Elements

In some kinds of magick and witchcraft, the four elements of earth, air, fire, and water play important roles in ritual and spell work. Each one is assigned a cardinal direction as well as universal energetic traits. These elements are viewed as alive and communicative, contributing energy to our workings. The thing is, each element has so many different ways of existing that it's difficult to paint them all with the same brush. Sometimes an element is helpful, like nourishing summer rain, and other times destructive, like a flood. These two things are both comprised of water but possess very different energies. It only makes sense that the form an element takes can have an impact on your magick, much like the phases of the moon do.

Next I've compiled some forms that each element can take. I also describe how the spirit of each element feels to me, and outline some ways they can be integrated into spells and rituals.

Fire

Fire invokes passion, transformation, anger, lust, and success. Fire is an unpredictable, wild element, and working with its spirit creates fast, sometimes overwhelming results. To capture the different spirits of fire, you can keep the ashes in envelopes and label where they came from.

CANDLE FLAME

A candle flame may be little, but it's got bite. A bright, tall candle flame indicates a strong, determined spirit, whereas a flickering flame suggests an unpredictable, erratic one. Perhaps it's undulating playfully in its movements or spitting as if angry. Since a small candle flame can potentially grow larger and spread (whether intentionally or accidentally), it seems to me to have a youthful spirit within it. Candle flames can be made to fit any spell. Watch how the flame behaves to determine the energy present.

BONFIRE

This form of fire is friendly, helpful, and cozy, with a mature, nurturing spirit. It can help to prepare food for sustenance but is also used to burn away unneeded things like yard waste. A bonfire does both at once, creating and destroying, which makes it an encouraging spirit of transition that urges you to grow. Sometimes the spirit of a bonfire exists solely to warm you lovingly, and other times it is a celebratory dancer. Pay attention and you might notice that the spirit of a bonfire mirrors the feelings of the people around it as if interacting with them. Bonfires are excellent in spells for friendship and community.

FOREST OR HOUSE FIRE

The most powerful fires are the destructive kind. They bring about huge, often devastating changes. These spirits may be those of rage, vengeance, and revolution. If you wish to work with the energy of destruction, find some ashes or an object that has been touched by the fire, and include it in your working. Just be careful what you wish for!

Air

The element of air represents intellect, communication, and wisdom. It's often included in workings regarding learning, sending messages, and travel. Working with air in spells is often dependent on the weather, so don't be afraid of spontaneity. When the wind calls, go work your magick.

Air represents intellect, communication, and wisdom. It's often included in workings regarding learning, sending messages, and travel....When the wind calls, go work your magick.

Breeze

A soft breeze is like a whisper of encouragement, carrying a spirit that wants to soothe and calm you. Feeling a breeze on your skin is like being patted gently by loving hands, or even held all over. The spirit within the breeze can bring comfort, cool you off, and offer a refreshing clearing of the mind. It's a sweet sort of spirit, reminding you that you're never alone. A steady wind carries the same sentiment but with more urgency, perhaps with the message that you need to move on from whatever is troubling you or make important changes.

Gusts

A sudden gust of wind can be alarming. The spirit within it is impatient. It wants to get your attention *now*, perhaps to relay a message. This kind of air spirit will tear around, knock things over, and take your breath away. Then it disappears as suddenly as it came. Like a temper tantrum, this spirit expresses itself passionately and quickly.

But like words that are shouted in a heightened emotional state, there can be permanent results. Including gusts of wind in your workings will have the same effect.

Fog

While some could argue that fog falls in the water category, I feel it belongs with the air element, as its movement depends on it. The spirit of fog is intuitive, encourages deep thought, and carries hidden information. When fog creeps in, it might seem ominous. Its spirit is otherworldly, obscures the conscious mind, and causes you to look inward and think differently than usual. Fog is the spirit of secrets kept and can be included in workings for uncovering that which cannot be seen.

Earth

The element of earth includes dirt, trees, and all plants. This means there is a wide range of materials that fall within this category, from flowers to animal bones. Earth represents stability, prosperity, and purpose. You can collect earth from various places and keep it in labeled jars for future use. This is especially beneficial when you visit someplace special.

Fertile Soil

Naturally fertile soil contains the spirit of growth, youth, and potential. This spirit is hopeful, healthy, and positive. It can cause things to grow, including ideas and projects, making it inspiring and motivational. It encourages physical and mental health and carries a reminder to live in the moment. Fresh soil is excellent for healing spells, fertility rites, and starting new ventures.

Dirt/Pebbles

Spirits within dirt and pebbles are as unique to their location as wild-life. Pebbles from a road contain the transient spirit of travel and wanderlust. Dirt from a playground might have a playful, childish spirit, whereas that from the property of a mansion is prosperous. Earth collected from the site of a disaster will contain destructive elements. Dirt can be collected from any location that's relevant to your goal and added to spell bottles, sachets, or even candle dressing.

Boulders

Large stones, ranging from boulders to mountains, are monolithic spirits of vitality and stability. Lying upon a boulder or expanse of stone will ground you, aligning you with the steady energy of the earth. These large spirits are older than any of us can imagine and contain the patience and wisdom of millennia. They are wise, all-knowing beings that move very slowly. They have survived and endured for so long that they never tire, but are consistent and reliable. They existed before we were born and they will exist when we are gone.

Water

The element of water is emotional, intuitive, and all about feelings. Water is included in many cleansing and purification rituals, love spells, and workings regarding the inner self. Collect water for spells by setting a jar outside during storms, scooping up some snow and letting it melt, or taking a sample from a river or lake.

Pond

If you look closely at a pond, you'll see it's a very lively place for insects and other critters. Its spirit is vivacious and beautiful. Flourishing with life and growth, frogs and bugs lay their eggs there. Ponds contain a creative spirit that encourages childlike wonder and daydreams. Still pond water is reflective like a mirror and can be included in spells for beauty and self-love. While you shouldn't drink water from ponds, you can add a little drop to your soap or beauty products to enhance confidence and encourage you to dream.

Rain

Whether a gentle drizzle or an all-out storm, rain possesses a cleansing, clearing spirit. Depending on the type of rain, it can be refreshing or ferocious. Accompanied by thunder and lightning, a storm has an aggressive, intimidating spirit. Mighty, awe-inspiring, and sometimes scary, it refuses to be overlooked. In magick, rain collected from a storm can give strong, commanding energy to your working. On the other hand, gentle rain tends to be soft and nourishing. When the ground is dry, rain comes with the spirit of giving as it relieves the parched earth. This type of rain can be included in spells for emotional health.

Snow

Snow is one of my favorite types of water to use in witchcraft because it has so many possibilities. The spirit of a soft, fluffy snowfall feels like a blanket settling over life, muting the noise of the world, bringing a sense of gratitude for simple things like a warm house and a comfy bed. The spirit within an ice storm, however, feels punishing, with its sharp pellets and resulting hydro outages and closed roads. While not necessarily nefarious, this type of storm does remind us of just how huge and powerful nature can be and that we are at its mercy. To include snow and ice in your spells, melt some in a container and store it for future use.

. . . .

These descriptions of spirits within the elements are based on my own experiences, so the way you interpret them may be different. There are many contributing factors to how you interact with different spirits, like location, history, their role in nature, and how you found it. Sometimes a spirit will make itself known to you in an obvious way, such as a feather falling from the sky into your path. Other times there is no purpose; we simply have the pleasure of coexisting with all the beautiful, diverse beings that make up the earth and the cosmos.

Every so often, take time to stop and be aware of the world around you. Allow yourself to feel, smell, and see the life in all things and how it mirrors your own. When you realize that all things are alive just like you, you realize that you are never truly alone.

Kate Freuler *lives in Ontario, Canada, and is the author of* Of Blood and Bones: Working with Shadow Magick & the Dark Moon. *She owns and operates White Moon Witchcraft, an online witchcraft boutique. When she isn't crafting spells and amulets for clients or herself, she loves to write, paint, read, draw, and create. Visit her at www.katefreuler.com.*

Illustrator: Bri Hermanson

Water Wellness Magick

Sapphire Moonbeam

Water is the original magical elixir. It sustains all of life. I believe water should be considered sacred and treated with the utmost care, especially since our lives depend on it. In nature, water demands our respect with the force of powerful storms. When water is revered with honor, this natural life force can help us with overall mind, body, and spirit wellness.

Water is the element in nature that represents and mirrors our emotions. It can be a peaceful flowing river, a pond

with small ripples, or a lake reflection in the evening under the light of the moon…as well as a powerful ocean wave, a rushing waterfall, swift bubbling river rapids, a flood, or treacherous storms and hurricanes. Since water relates to our emotions, it can be used in our magical practice to assist with determination and transformation.

Combining the Elements

Water can be combined with the other natural elements to help create desired outcomes in our magical practice. I have a few suggestions for your magical practice; however, the creative details you add and your reasons for using water in your magick are entirely up to you. A spell with water and fire can be used to "heat up" a situation you are passionate about working on and manifesting. Alternatively, water can be used to douse a flame and make something that has overheated and gotten out of control cool off and become less fiery. Frozen water can be used to influence a situation in your life to slow down or potentially make it stop.

When water is added to earth for nourishment of seeds, it helps a project grow. When salt is added, water can also be used for protection. Combining water with the air element can be used in spells to create movement. You can use the power of visualization to think about rainfall, a waterspout, or a thunderstorm as an aid in your water magick. You can find unique ways to use the elements of nature with water in your magical practice to achieve your desired result.

Water and Magick

In the early days of my magical path, I became enamored with the idea of making moon water under the radiant light of the full moon. The moon and its rays are quite powerful. The moon affects the oceans and the tides, so it can certainly influence moon water with that same energy. Moon water can be infused with your intentions and then used in a house blessing, a ritual bath, or cleansing stones and crystals, as well as for watering plants and herbs to be used in a future spell. There are endless ways that water can assist in our magical practice.

I use water every day in my own life to help restore balance and facilitate overall wellness. As a water sign myself, one of my favorite things to do is to soak in the evenings in a hot bath in the clawfoot tub in my 1920s house. I know some people prefer showers, but I hope to convince shower lovers to consider utilizing the restorative, healing, and magical benefits that can be gained from being submerged in healing water.

Of course we use water to clean and purify ourselves, but we can also use water to make magical concoctions for spells. If you are in a household that is not supportive of your magical path, or if you just want to practice magick in a place of solitude for any reason, the bath is perfect for that. Immersing yourself in water that is filled with your own magical intentions, scents, herbs, oils, and different types of soap is a wonderful way to literally soak up the magick.

My Bathhouse Experience

The Greeks and Romans built elaborate bath houses in ancient times. In addition to bathing and healing, the bath houses became a place to gather as a community for socializing and networking. The people of Turkey also built a type of public steam bath called a hammam, dating back to the Ottoman Empire in the late thirteenth century.

When I visited Istanbul a few years ago, I was able to spend time at a Turkish bath house with the women's spiritual retreat group I was traveling with. The building itself was elaborate and elegant. It was filled with carved marble and high ceilings. As I waited for my turn to bathe, I rested on my back on a large heated marble bench. I was a bit apprehensive about bathing in a group, but it turned out to be more of a spa type of experience. We each had an attendant who helped to wash and massage us separately. It was a wonderful experience. I felt like I was being pampered and treated like a goddess.

Self-Care, Energy, and Protection

Back at home in the United States, no matter what the day brings, I can soak in my clawfoot tub and make everything in my life stop. Bathing is a great way to relax and focus on the present moment. As I wrote in one of my spells for Llewellyn's 2023 Witches' Spell-A-Day Almanac regarding suggestions for making an herbal bath tea, hot water helps to stimulate blood flow, lowers blood pressure, and eases pain in muscles and joints. Bathing in hot water also helps to increase your oxygen intake. Research has shown that soaking in hot water for ten minutes a day can help with depression and anxiety. A hot bath contributes to an overall sense of wellbeing and helps our bodies rest more easily at night.

Soaking in hot water for ten minutes a day can help with depression and anxiety. A hot bath contributes to an overall sense of wellbeing and helps our bodies rest more easily at night.

I use bathing in my magical practice in several ways. When I want to pamper myself, I take the time to add extra elements to my nightly bath for self-care. I love the scent of roses and like to use rose petals in my bath. Sometimes I create my own rose water with the petals. Any time you create your own bath products, the effects are more powerful than from store-bought supplies. However, if you don't have that kind of time, rose water can be purchased from stores. If you like the scent of a different flower, use what you prefer. My self-love bath also includes white candles for peace and pink candles for self-compassion. I also like to place rose quartz crystals and quartz crystals near my clawfoot tub. Bath teas, scented soap, herbs, and essential oils are additional ways to create an atmosphere of peace.

A lot has been written in recent years about people who are described as empaths. While I do think this information is helpful, I believe that anyone with an increased sense of self-awareness regarding energy can benefit from soaking in water once a day. I prefer a nightly bath so I can cleanse my energetic aura field and wash away extra energy I have picked up during the day. Water helps me refresh and renew my physical energy as well as revitalize my personal energy field.

I prefer a nightly bath so I can cleanse my energetic aura field and wash away extra energy I have picked up during the day. Water helps me refresh and renew my physical energy as well as revitalize my personal energy field.

When I take a bath for the protection of my energy, I use a combination of salts. Epsom salt helps with therapeutic benefits. While it isn't actually a salt (but rather a pure mineral compound of magnesium sulfate in crystal form), it is easily found in stores and helps soothe sore muscles and joints. I use a combination of Epsom salt and sea salts for protection and restorative benefits. I sometimes add a small amount of black salt for additional magical protection.

I have made my own magical bath salts for my bath time. I combine the salts and add a tiny bit of color and fragrant scents. I place the bath salts in beautiful containers that I decorate with sparkly elements. You can easily make a mixture of your own salts for the bath. While stirring the salt mixture into your bath, consciously add love and protection to it, as well as energies for luck or success.

Ritual Bath

A ritual bath can be taken before attending a full moon ceremony, a sabbat, or a new moon ritual. There are different ways to take a ritual bath. You can use cold water instead of hot to energize your skin. Cold water invigorates your system and can increase your adrenaline, making you feel more lively before the ritual begins. I prefer hot baths. For a ritual bath, I sit in the tub and stay there until the water completely drains around me. The change from the hot water to a lower temperature on my body as the water slowly drains provides a sensation that makes me feel physically ready as I prepare for the ritual.

Meditation in the Bath

Sometimes I use my evening bath for meditation. I really enjoy meditating, but sometimes I don't have enough time for it during the day. When I take my relaxing bath, it helps slow my thoughts and I can ease into a meditative state. More than once when I have been soaking in my clawfoot tub with my eyes closed, I have suddenly experienced some incredible inspiration or eureka moment. The ideas seem to magically appear in my thoughts. It is as if I didn't have access to this information during the day because I was too busy or too tense. Slowing down and meditating in the bathwater, either in silence or while listening to instrumental music, helps my innermost thoughts and creative ideas flow effortlessly and easily.

Water and Astrology

If you love astrology and are familiar with your personal birth chart, take a look at it to see if you have an imbalance in the elements represented by the horoscope signs. If your birth chart lacks the element of earth, fire, water, or air, consider using a magical bath to add more of that specific element to your bath. You can add earth energy by using more bath salts. To add more of the fire element, safely burn extra candles during your bath time. To add more of the air element, recite spiritual mantras, sing, or listen to music or guided meditations while bathing. The bathwater itself naturally adds more water for balance, along with the benefits I have already described.

. . . .

Magick is what you make. Use your creativity and consider taking more magical baths to manifest your desires in addition to self-care. Water is a powerful element that we can rely on daily for balance in our mind, body, and spirit. Water is the original magical elixir.

Sapphire Moonbeam *is a rainbow energy artist, metaphysical jewelry maker, card reader, nature photographer, and nature lover. She is the artist and author of the* Moonbeam Magick *oracle card deck. Sapphire sells her artwork, jewelry, and oracle deck online and teaches intuitive abstract art classes at locations around the world. She has a worldwide following at her Sapphire's Moonbeams page on Facebook. Visit SapphireMoonbeam.com.*

Illustrator: Tim Foley

The Sustainable Witch

Tudorbeth

Sustainability is a common buzzword in our world, yet what exactly does it mean? Sustainability means living in balance and harmony not only with the environment but economically and socially as well. As witches, this is essentially what we do and have done for centuries. The best way to describe the sustainable path of a witch is by explaining how to celebrate the festivals on the Wheel of the Year in an environmentally, economically, and socially balanced way.

Yule

I think that Yule is probably the hardest of festivals to celebrate sustainably due to the very nature of the gift-giving practice of the season. Yule falls just before Christmas, an incredibly commercial and money-driven holiday. If there are members of your extended family who do not adhere to your magical practice, this can become a very strained and expensive month. However, there are several practical things you can do to make your practices more sustainable.

For all the festivals on the Wheel of the Year, always go straight to your grimoire or book of shadows and break down the festival itself. For example, write at the top of your page "Yule/Imbolc/Ostara," then underneath list the practical tasks involved, for example, decorations, meals, etc. Then break those tasks down into sustainable practices.

Yule is usually symbolized by the Yule tree, and millions of pine trees around the world are destroyed each year due to this practice. For a more sustainable practice, buy a tree with roots. This could even be a small tabletop tree. Each year after the twelve days of Yule have finished and the decorations come down, replant the tree into a larger pot and leave it outdoors, caring for it as you would other plants. The following Yule, bring the tree indoors again. When it becomes too big to plant in a pot and too heavy to move, plant it in the ground, giving thanks. Then start all over again with another little tree.

It is not just the pine tree that represents nature and Yule. Ivy and of course the holly tree are also symbolic of this time of year. An ivy plant or holly tree can be brought into the house and given centre stage for the festival of Yule. I personally do not like to cut plants and prefer to keep the living roots connected, so I have plants that I bring into the house for that celebration. Though many people do cut sprigs of holly and ivy, to be completely sustainable, simply do not do this.

Another tradition at this time of year, and one of the most popular, is the act of giving presents. This is where sustainability and social expectations come to the fore, but with careful planning they do not need be in competition with each other. The sustainable path is one in which creativity and imagination take precedence, and finding an alternative way to celebrate a tradition can be fun.

Instead of buying gifts at Yule, have each member of the family write their name on a little piece of paper. Then fold up the papers and place them in a hat or Yule log. Have each member randomly take a name from the hat or log. For the whole month of December or the twelve days of Yule, they do something every day for that named person, and that is their gift.

Imbolc

Imbolc is all about the light returning to the earth once more and is probably one of my favourite festivals. It comes first in the calendar year, on the 2nd of February, and signifies the beginning of the end of winter.

To celebrate Imbolc sustainably, plant some snowdrops in a little pot that you can use every year. Make a white candle with either vanilla or myrrh oil. The herbs can be basil, bay, or rosemary. As you light your candle, say:

> Welcome to the quickening of the earth,
> Heralding the coming spring.
> Blessed be to one and all.
> Welcome to the light you bring.

Furthermore, as it is almost spring, it is time to start cleaning! Clear out cupboards and drawers, places that are traditionally dark and do not see the light. Move energy and light around and give your home a freshen up.

Ostara

Ostara falls on the spring equinox, when day and night are of equal length, and is the time when we plant the seeds that were gathered at the last harvest as part of the ritual celebration.

For your altar, decorate with spring flowers, such as daffodils and narcissi, in pots that can be placed outside for the rest of the year. Make a yellow altar candle with lily of the valley, jasmine, marjoram, honeysuckle, or lemon oil as well as the flowers and herbs.

This is also the time when you could begin to clear out your winter wardrobe to make space for lighter clothes. I always like to have an Ostara wardrobe party, where friends and family swap clothes and take the unwanted items to a thrift store.

Beltane

Beltane falls on April 30th or May Day (the 1st of May) and is known as the "fire festival" due to the bonfires that are lit. It is also the spring festival of merrymaking and has long been a celebration of fertility and dancing, notably around the Maypole.

I celebrate all spring, summer, and autumn festivals outside, and it is only for the winter ones that I bring nature indoors in the form of a plant or tree. To celebrate Beltane, make a red candle with peach oil and marigold flowers and perform a ribbon spell, which represents the ancient Maypole ribbons that our ancestors danced around.

Litha

The summer solstice is when the sun is at its height and is the longest day of the year. Fairies, pixies, and all manner of elementals are known to be active at this time. Handmade candles can be two-tone, with orange and white (white for the white heat of the sun). The oils and herbs used can be bay, chamomile, fennel, lavender, or orange blossom. St. John's wort was traditionally picked on this day, and I like to gather herbs to make into sage/herb sticks as part of my celebrations.

At this time of year there are usually plenty of fresh fruits and vegetables available, notably strawberries. If you cannot grow them, then attending a pick-your-own farm is a wonderful sustainable tradition to begin for Litha.

I like strawberry pancakes with maple syrup, a very simple dessert. Make the pancake mix with 5 tablespoons of plain flour, 3 eggs, and a half pint (or 300 milliliters) of milk. (Rice or soy milk is fine.) Mix the ingredients together, and have a punnet (carton) of strawberries washed and chopped up in quarters. Add the strawberries to the pancake batter and cook, making sure to have a hot frying pan. Serve hot with lots of maple syrup and enjoy.

Lammas

Lammas is the first festival of the harvest—a clear indication that autumn is on its way. Lammas is usually represented by wheat, so loaves of bread, corn dollies, and sunflowers (which are out in abundance in August) all represent this festival. On August 1, I simply light a yellow candle dressed with basil essential oil or a few drops of sunflower oil and say:

> Blessed be to one and all.
> I acknowledge the changing season
> And embrace the autumn's call.

Have a glass of wine or beer with your bread and dinner. Savour every taste and give thanks for the harvest and the food you eat.

Mabon

I love Mabon, as it is one of the most powerful days of the year and is the start of autumn. The leaves start to turn and city parks become a canvas of colours. It is traditionally a good time to enact rituals for protection and security, so cast a money spell or a career enhancement spell.

Make a two-tone candle of black and white and use almond, apple, or rosemary essential oil. I also make my own facial mask with oatmeal and yoghurt, as oats are another symbol of this festival and turn Mabon into a contemplation and relaxation festival in preparation for the winter.

[Mabon] is traditionally a good time to enact rituals for protection and security, so cast a money spell or a career enhancement spell.

This face mask is easy to make and suitable for all skin types (although do a patch-test first). Use one tablespoon of oatmeal finely ground, one tablespoon of plain organic yogurt, and a teaspoon of honey. Combine the ingredients in a small bowl, mixing well. Then apply the mask to your face for about ten minutes before washing it off with warm water and applying your moisturizer as normal.

Samhain

Samhain, on October 31, is a time of divination. One of my favourite traditions is to catch a falling leaf before it reaches the ground and make a wish upon it. The ones I catch I usually keep on my altar for the coming year to see when each wish comes true.

Begin a Samhain/Halloween tradition of serving up the Mash O' Nine Sorts. This is a traditional Samhain dish that is served to unmarried guests, in which a ring is hidden. Of course, whoever finds the ring will be married next.

To make Mash O' Nine Sorts, you need 400 grams (1½ cups) of potatoes, two carrots, a turnip and a parsnip, two leeks, 100 grams (¾ cup) of peas, salt and pepper, and a carton of single cream (or half-and-half). Prepare and boil all the vegetables, then mash together the potatoes, carrots, turnip, and parsnip. Season with salt and pepper. Add the sliced leeks and mix in some of the cream, then stir in the peas and a ring. Transfer to an ovenproof dish and cook at moderate heat (350°F/180°C) until golden brown. Make sure you warn people about the ring before they start eating just in case! Serve pumpkin pie for dessert. Divination at Samhain can be tasty.

Tudorbeth *is a hereditary practitioner of witchcraft. Her great-grandmother was a famous tea reader in Ireland, while her Welsh great-grandmother knew every plant and food in nature. She has a BA honours degree in religious studies and an MA in medieval studies from the University of Lincoln and is currently researching her PhD. Tudorbeth writes for many publications and is a regular contributor to magazines. She has written many books, including the* The Hedgewitch's Little Book of Spells, Charms & Brews *and* The Hedgewitch's Little Book of Seasonal Magic (*both for Llewellyn*) *and* A Spellbook for All Seasons: Welcome Natural Change with Magical Blessings (*Eddison Books*). *She is on Twitter @Tudorbeth and also Instagram @Tudorbeth7, where she regularly posts spells and magical recipes.*

Illustrator: Tim Foley

The Lunar Calendar

September 2023 to December 2024

SEPTEMBER

S	M	T	W	T	F	S
					1	2
3	4	5	6	7	8	9
10	11	12	13	14	15	16
17	18	19	20	21	22	23
24	25	26	27	28	29	30

OCTOBER

S	M	T	W	T	F	S
1	2	3	4	5	6	7
8	9	10	11	12	13	14
15	16	17	18	19	20	21
22	23	24	25	26	27	28
29	30	31				

NOVEMBER

S	M	T	W	T	F	S
			1	2	3	4
5	6	7	8	9	10	11
12	13	14	15	16	17	18
19	20	21	22	23	24	25
26	27	28	29	30		

DECEMBER

S	M	T	W	T	F	S
					1	2
3	4	5	6	7	8	9
10	11	12	13	14	15	16
17	18	19	20	21	22	23
24	25	26	27	28	29	30
31						

2024

JANUARY

S	M	T	W	T	F	S
	1	2	3	4	5	6
7	8	9	10	11	12	13
14	15	16	17	18	19	20
21	22	23	24	25	26	27
28	29	30	31			

FEBRUARY

S	M	T	W	T	F	S
				1	2	3
4	5	6	7	8	9	10
11	12	13	14	15	16	17
18	19	20	21	22	23	24
25	26	27	28	29		

MARCH

S	M	T	W	T	F	S
					1	2
3	4	5	6	7	8	9
10	11	12	13	14	15	16
17	18	19	20	21	22	23
24	25	26	27	28	29	30
31						

APRIL

S	M	T	W	T	F	S
	1	2	3	4	5	6
7	8	9	10	11	12	13
14	15	16	17	18	19	20
21	22	23	24	25	26	27
28	29	30				

MAY

S	M	T	W	T	F	S
			1	2	3	4
5	6	7	8	9	10	11
12	13	14	15	16	17	18
19	20	21	22	23	24	25
26	27	28	29	30	31	

JUNE

S	M	T	W	T	F	S
						1
2	3	4	5	6	7	8
9	10	11	12	13	14	15
16	17	18	19	20	21	22
23	24	25	26	27	28	29
30						

JULY

S	M	T	W	T	F	S
	1	2	3	4	5	6
7	8	9	10	11	12	13
14	15	16	17	18	19	20
21	22	23	24	25	26	27
28	29	30	31			

AUGUST

S	M	T	W	T	F	S
				1	2	3
4	5	6	7	8	9	10
11	12	13	14	15	16	17
18	19	20	21	22	23	24
25	26	27	28	29	30	31

SEPTEMBER

S	M	T	W	T	F	S
1	2	3	4	5	6	7
8	9	10	11	12	13	14
15	16	17	18	19	20	21
22	23	24	25	26	27	28
29	30					

OCTOBER

S	M	T	W	T	F	S
		1	2	3	4	5
6	7	8	9	10	11	12
13	14	15	16	17	18	19
20	21	22	23	24	25	26
27	28	29	30	31		

NOVEMBER

S	M	T	W	T	F	S
					1	2
3	4	5	6	7	8	9
10	11	12	13	14	15	16
17	18	19	20	21	22	23
24	25	26	27	28	29	30

DECEMBER

S	M	T	W	T	F	S
1	2	3	4	5	6	7
8	9	10	11	12	13	14
15	16	17	18	19	20	21
22	23	24	25	26	27	28
29	30	31				

SEPTEMBER 2023

SU	M	T	W
27	28	29	30
3 3rd ♈ ☽ v/c 7:57 am ☽ → ♉ 11:00 am ♀ D 9:20 pm	**4** 3rd ♉ ♃ Rx 10:10 am *Labor Day*	**5** 3rd ♉ ☽ v/c 12:46 pm ☽ → ♊ 4:07 pm	**●** 3rd ♊ 4th Quarter 6:21 pm
10 4th ♋ ☽ v/c 8:47 am ☽ → ♌ 12:36 pm	**11** 4th ♌	**12** 4th ♌ ☽ v/c 11:06 am	**13** 4th ♌ ☽ → ♍ 1:18 am
17 1st ♎ ☽ v/c 9:06 pm	**18** 1st ♎ ☽ → ♏ 12:58 am	**19** 1st ♏	**20** 1st ♏ ☽ v/c 6:21 am ☽ → ♐ 10:06 am
24 2nd ♑ ☽ v/c 4:05 pm ☽ → ♒ 7:29 pm	**25** 2nd ♒	**26** 2nd ♒ ☽ v/c 8:38 am ☽ → ♓ 8:18 pm	**27** 2nd ♓
1	2	3	4

Eastern Daylight Time (EDT)

ZODIAC SIGNS

♈ Aries	♌ Leo	♐ Sagittarius
♉ Taurus	♍ Virgo	♑ Capricorn
♊ Gemini	♎ Libra	♒ Aquarius
♋ Cancer	♏ Scorpio	♓ Pisces

PLANETS

☉ Sun	♃ Jupiter
☽ Moon	♄ Saturn
☿ Mercury	♅ Uranus
♀ Venus	♆ Neptune
♂ Mars	♇ Pluto

SEPTEMBER 2023

TH	F	SA	NOTES
31	3rd ♓ 1 ☽ v/c 6:36 am ☽ → ♈ 9:25 am	3rd ♈ 2	
4th ♊ 7 ☽ v/c 6:22 pm	4th ♊ 8 ☽ → ♋ 1:00 am	4th ♋ 9	
4th ♍ ● New Moon 9:40 pm *New Moon*	1st ♍ 15 ☽ v/c 9:49 am ☽ → ♎ 1:44 pm ☿ D 4:21 pm *Mercury direct*	1st ♎ 16	
1st ♐ 21	1st ♐ ◐ ☽ v/c 3:32 pm 2nd Quarter 3:32 pm ☽ → ♑ 4:20 pm	2nd ♑ 23 ☉ → ♎ 2:50 am *Mabon* *Sun enters Libra* *Fall Equinox*	
2nd ♓ 28 ☽ v/c 4:58 pm ☽ → ♈ 8:17 pm	2nd ♈ 29 Full Moon 5:58 am *Harvest Moon*	3rd ♈ 30 ☽ v/c 5:50 pm ☽ → ♉ 9:18 pm	
5	6	7	

ASPECTS & MOON PHASES

☌ Conjunction	0°	● New Moon	(1st Quarter)
⚹ Sextile	60°	◐ Waxing Moon	(2nd Quarter)
☐ Square	90°	○ Full Moon	(3rd Quarter)
△ Trine	120°	◑ Waning Moon	(4th Quarter)
⚻ Quincunx	150°		
☍ Opposition	180°		

OCTOBER 2023

SU	M	T	W
1 3rd ♉	**2** 3rd ♉ ☽ v/c 9:20 pm	**3** 3rd ♉ ☽ → ♊ 1:03 am	**4** 3rd ♊ ☿ → ♎ 8:09 pm
8 4th ♌ ♀ → ♍ 9:11 pm	**9** 4th ♌	**10** 4th ♌ ☽ v/c 5:37 am ☽ → ♍ 8:02 am ♀ D 9:10 pm	**11** 4th ♍
15 1st ♎ ☽ v/c 3:01 am ☽ → ♏ 7:04 am	**16** 1st ♏	**17** 1st ♏ ☽ v/c 11:44 am ☽ → ♐ 3:36 pm	**18** 1st ♐
22 2nd ♑ ☽ v/c 2:00 am ☽ → ♒ 2:06 am ☿ → ♏ 2:49 am	**23** 2nd ♒ ☉ → ♏ 12:21 pm ☽ v/c 3:04 pm *Sun enters Scorpio*	**24** 2nd ♒ ☽ → ♓ 4:33 am	**25** 2nd ♓
29 3rd ♉	**30** 3rd ♉ ☽ v/c 7:36 am ☽ → ♊ 11:08 am	**31** 3rd ♊ *Samhain* *Halloween*	**1**
5	**6**	**7**	**8**

Eastern Daylight Time (EDT)

Zodiac Signs

♈ Aries	♌ Leo	♐ Sagittarius
♉ Taurus	♍ Virgo	♑ Capricorn
♊ Gemini	♎ Libra	♒ Aquarius
♋ Cancer	♏ Scorpio	♓ Pisces

Planets

☉ Sun	♃ Jupiter
☽ Moon	♄ Saturn
☿ Mercury	♅ Uranus
♀ Venus	♆ Neptune
♂ Mars	♇ Pluto

OCTOBER 2023

TH	F	SA	NOTES
5 3rd ♊ ☽ v/c 2:34 am ☽ → ♋ 8:32 am	**6** 3rd ♋ 4th Quarter 9:48 am ◑	**7** 4th ♋ ☽ v/c 3:12 pm ☽ → ♌ 7:24 pm	
12 4th ♍ ♂ → ♏ 12:04 am ☽ v/c 4:10 pm ☽ → ♎ 8:22 pm	**13** 4th ♎	**14** 4th ♎ New Moon 1:55 pm ● *Solar Eclipse/ New Moon*	
19 1st ♐ ☽ v/c 3:02 pm ☽ → ♑ 9:55 pm	**20** 1st ♑	**21** 1st ♑ 2nd Quarter 11:29 pm ◑	
26 2nd ♓ ☽ v/c 2:39 am ☽ → ♈ 6:02 am	**27** 2nd ♈	**28** 2nd ♈ ☽ v/c 4:20 am ☽ → ♉ 7:44 am Full Moon 4:24 pm ○ *Lunar Eclipse/ Blood Moon*	
2	3	4	
9	10	11	

ASPECTS & MOON PHASES

☌ Conjunction	0°	● New Moon	(1st Quarter)
✶ Sextile	60°	◑ Waxing Moon	(2nd Quarter)
☐ Square	90°	○ Full Moon	(3rd Quarter)
△ Trine	120°	◑ Waning Moon	(4th Quarter)
⚻ Quincunx	150°		
☍ Opposition	180°		

NOVEMBER 2023

SU	M	T	W
29	30	31	3rd ♊ ☽ v/c 8:36 am ☽ → ♋ 5:30 pm **1**
3rd ♌ EST in effect 2:00 am 4th Quarter 3:37 am ◑ **5** *Daylight Saving Time ends at 2:00 am*	4th ♌ **6** ☽ v/c 2:25 am ☽ → ♍ 2:39 pm	4th ♍ **7** *Election Day (general)*	4th ♍ **8** ♀ → ♎ 4:30 am ☽ v/c 11:55 pm
4th ♏ **12**	4th ♏ ● **13** New Moon 4:27 am ☽ v/c 6:03 pm ☽ → ♐ 9:23 pm *New Moon*	1st ♐ **14**	1st ♐ **15** ☽ v/c 5:57 pm
1st ♒ **19**	1st ♒ ◐ **20** ☽ v/c 5:50 am 2nd Quarter 5:50 am ☽ → ♓ 9:29 am	2nd ♓ **21**	2nd ♓ **22** ☉ → ♐ 9:03 am ☽ v/c 10:10 am ☽ → ♈ 12:19 pm *Sun enters Sagittarius*
2nd ♉ **26** ☽ v/c 4:52 pm ☽ → ♊ 7:40 pm	2nd ♊ ○ **27** Full Moon 4:16 am *Mourning Moon*	3rd ♊ **28** ☽ v/c 8:03 pm	3rd ♊ **29** ☽ → ♋ 1:54 am
3	4	5	6

Eastern Daylight Time (EDT) becomes Eastern Standard Time (EST) November 5

NOVEMBER 2023

TH	F	SA	NOTES
3rd ⊗ **2**	3rd ⊗ **3** ☽ v/c 11:28 pm	3rd ⊗ **4** ♄ D 3:03 am ☽ → ♌ 3:21 am	
4th ♍ **9** ☽ → ♎ 3:08 am	4th ♎ **10** ☿ → ♐ 1:25 am	4th ♎ **11** ☽ v/c 10:05 am ☽ → ♏ 1:39 pm *Veterans Day*	
1st ♐ **16** ☽ → ♑ 2:41 am	1st ♑ **17**	1st ♑ **18** ☽ v/c 3:27 am ☽ → ♒ 6:28 am	
2nd ♈ **23** *Thanksgiving Day*	2nd ♈ **24** ♂ → ♐ 5:15 am ☽ v/c 12:40 pm ☽ → ♉ 3:29 pm	2nd ♉ **25**	
3rd ⊗ **30**	**1**	**2**	
7	**8**	**9**	

ASPECTS & MOON PHASES

♂ Conjunction	0°	● New Moon	(1st Quarter)
✶ Sextile	60°	◑ Waxing Moon	(2nd Quarter)
▢ Square	90°	○ Full Moon	(3rd Quarter)
△ Trine	120°	◐ Waning Moon	(4th Quarter)
⚻ Quincunx	150°		
☍ Opposition	180°		

DECEMBER 2023

SU	M	T	W
26	27	28	29
3 3rd ♌ ☽ v/c 9:11 pm ☽ → ♍ 10:50 pm	**4** 3rd ♍ ♀ → ♏ 1:51 pm	**28** 3rd ♍ 4th Quarter 12:49 am ◑	**6** 4th ♍ ♆ D 8:20 am ☽ v/c 8:50 am ☽ → ♎ 11:35 am
10 4th ♏	**11** 4th ♏ ☽ v/c 3:57 am ☽ → ♐ 6:11 am	**12** 4th ♐ New Moon 6:32 pm ● New Moon	**13** 1st ♐ ☽ v/c 1:48 am ☿ ℞ 2:09 am ☽ → ♑ 10:31 am Mercury retrograde
17 1st ♒ ☽ v/c 7:04 am ☽ → ♓ 2:58 pm	**18** 1st ♓	**19** 1st ♓ 2nd Quarter 1:39 pm ◐ ☽ v/c 4:03 pm ☽ → ♈ 5:47 pm	**20** 2nd ♈
24 2nd ♉ ☽ v/c 1:40 am ☽ → ♊ 3:15 am Christmas Eve	**25** 2nd ♊ Christmas Day	**26** 2nd ♊ ☽ v/c 2:55 am ☽ → ♋ 10:15 am Full Moon 7:33 pm ○ Kwanzaa begins Long Nights Moon	**27** 3rd ♋
31 3rd ♌ ☽ v/c 12:18 am ☽ → ♍ 6:53 am New Year's Eve	1	2	3

Eastern Standard Time (EST)

ZODIAC SIGNS

♈ Aries	♌ Leo	♐ Sagittarius
♉ Taurus	♍ Virgo	♑ Capricorn
♊ Gemini	♎ Libra	♒ Aquarius
♋ Cancer	♏ Scorpio	♓ Pisces

PLANETS

☉ Sun	♃ Jupiter
☽ Moon	♄ Saturn
☿ Mercury	♅ Uranus
♀ Venus	♆ Neptune
♂ Mars	♇ Pluto

DECEMBER 2023

TH	F	SA	NOTES
30	1 — 3rd ⊗ ☽ v/c 8:07 am ☿ → ♑ 9:31 am ☽ → ♌ 11:00 am	2 — 3rd ♌	
7 — 4th ♎	8 — 4th ♎ ☽ v/c 8:05 pm ☽ → ♏ 10:35 pm	9 — 4th ♏	
14 — 1st ♑	15 — 1st ♑ ☽ v/c 11:04 am ☽ → ♒ 12:56 pm	16 — 1st ♒	
21 — 2nd ♈ ☽ v/c 9:47 pm ☽ → ♉ 9:50 pm ☉ → ♑ 10:27 pm *Yule* *Sun enters Capricorn* *Winter Solstice*	22 — 2nd ♉	23 — 2nd ♉ ☿ → ♐ 1:18 am	
28 — 3rd ⊗ ☽ v/c 5:57 pm ☽ → ♌ 7:23 pm	29 — 3rd ♌ ♀ → ♐ 3:24 pm	30 — 3rd ♌ ♃ D 9:40 pm	
4	5	6	

ASPECTS & MOON PHASES

☌ Conjunction	0°	● New Moon	(1st Quarter)
⚹ Sextile	60°	◐ Waxing Moon	(2nd Quarter)
□ Square	90°	○ Full Moon	(3rd Quarter)
△ Trine	120°	◑ Waning Moon	(4th Quarter)
⚻ Quincunx	150°		
☍ Opposition	180°		

JANUARY 2024

SU	M	T	W
31	**1** 3rd ♍ ☿ D 10:08 pm *New Year's Day* *Kwanzaa ends* *Mercury direct*	**2** 3rd ♍ ☽ v/c 6:36 pm ☽ → ♎ 7:47 pm	**3** 3rd ♎ ◐ 4th Quarter 10:30 pm
7 4th ♏ ☽ v/c 3:22 pm ☽ → ♐ 4:08 pm	**8** 4th ♐	**9** 4th ♐ ☽ v/c 1:24 pm ☽ → ♑ 8:33 pm	**10** 4th ♑
14 1st ♓	**15** 1st ♓ ☽ v/c 11:33 pm ☽ → ♈ 11:49 pm *Martin Luther King Jr. Day*	**16** 1st ♈	**17** 1st ♈ ◑ 2nd Quarter 10:53 pm
21 2nd ♊	**22** 2nd ♊ ☽ v/c 3:40 pm ☽ → ♋ 4:51 pm	**23** 2nd ♋ ♀ → ♑ 3:50 am	**24** 2nd ♋ ☽ v/c 5:58 pm
28 3rd ♍	**29** 3rd ♍ ☽ v/c 6:20 pm	**30** 3rd ♍ ☽ → ♎ 3:04 am	**31** 3rd ♎
4	5	6	7

Eastern Standard Time (EST)

ZODIAC SIGNS

♈ Aries	♌ Leo	♐ Sagittarius
♉ Taurus	♍ Virgo	♑ Capricorn
♊ Gemini	♎ Libra	♒ Aquarius
♋ Cancer	♏ Scorpio	♓ Pisces

PLANETS

☉ Sun	♃ Jupiter
☽ Moon	♄ Saturn
☿ Mercury	♅ Uranus
♀ Venus	♆ Neptune
♂ Mars	♇ Pluto

JANUARY 2024

TH	F	SA	NOTES
4th ♎ **4** ♂ → ♑ 9:58 am	4th ♎ **5** ☽ v/c 6:41 am ☽ → ♏ 7:39 am	4th ♏ **6**	
4th ♑ ● New Moon 6:57 am ☽ v/c 9:33 pm ☽ → ♒ 10:01 pm *New Moon*	1st ♒ **12**	1st ♒ **13** ☽ v/c 4:59 am ☿ → ♑ 9:49 pm ☽ → ♓ 10:29 pm	
2nd ♈ **18** ☽ v/c 3:03 am ☽ → ♉ 3:12 am	2nd ♉ **19**	2nd ♉ **20** ☽ v/c 8:57 am ☽ → ♊ 8:58 am ☉ → ♒ 9:07 am ♇ → ♒ 7:50 pm *Sun enters Aquarius*	
2nd ♋ ○ ☽ → ♌ 2:37 am Full Moon 12:54 pm *Cold Moon*	3rd ♌ **26** ☽ v/c 4:19 pm	3rd ♌ **27** ♅ D 2:35 am ☽ → ♍ 2:11 pm	
1	2	3	
8	9	10	

Aspects & Moon Phases

☌ Conjunction	0°	● New Moon	(1st Quarter)
⚹ Sextile	60°	◐ Waxing Moon	(2nd Quarter)
□ Square	90°	○ Full Moon	(3rd Quarter)
△ Trine	120°	◑ Waning Moon	(4th Quarter)
⚻ Quincunx	150°		
☍ Opposition	180°		

FEBRUARY 2024

SU	M	T	W
28	**29**	**30**	**31**
4 4th ♏ ☽ → ♐ 1:28 am	**5** 4th ♐ ☿ → ≈ 12:10 am	**6** 4th ♐ ☽ v/c 12:06 am ☽ → ♑ 7:08 am	**7** 4th ♑
11 1st ♓	**12** 1st ♓ ☽ v/c 7:32 am ☽ → ♈ 8:26 am	**13** 1st ♈ ♂ → ≈ 1:05 am _Mardi Gras (Fat Tuesday)_	**14** 1st ♈ ☽ v/c 5:21 am ☽ → ♉ 10:02 am _Valentine's Day_ _Ash Wednesday_
18 2nd ♊ ☽ v/c 10:21 pm ☽ → ♋ 10:25 pm ☉ → ♓ 11:13 pm _Sun enters Pisces_	**19** 2nd ♋ _Presidents' Day_	**20** 2nd ♋	**21** 2nd ♋ ☽ v/c 1:38 am ☽ → ♌ 8:40 am
25 3rd ♍	**26** 3rd ♍ ☽ v/c 2:35 am ☽ → ♎ 9:29 am	**27** 3rd ♎ ☽ v/c 1:22 pm	**28** 3rd ♎ ☽ → ♏ 10:09 pm
3	**4**	**5**	**6**

Eastern Standard Time (EST)

ZODIAC SIGNS

♈ Aries	♌ Leo	♐ Sagittarius
♉ Taurus	♍ Virgo	♑ Capricorn
♊ Gemini	♎ Libra	≈ Aquarius
♋ Cancer	♏ Scorpio	♓ Pisces

PLANETS

☉ Sun	♃ Jupiter
☽ Moon	♄ Saturn
☿ Mercury	♅ Uranus
♀ Venus	♆ Neptune
♂ Mars	♇ Pluto

FEBRUARY 2024

TH	F	SA	NOTES
3rd ♎︎ **1** ☽ v/c 4:03 am ☽ → ♏︎ 3:37 pm	3rd ♏︎ ◑ 4th Quarter 6:18 pm *Imbolc* *Groundhog Day*	4th ♏︎ **3** ☽ v/c 10:24 pm	
4th ♑︎ **8** ☽ v/c 2:52 am ☽ → ♒︎ 8:59 am	4th ♒︎ ● ☽ v/c 5:59 pm New Moon 5:59 pm *New Moon*	1st ♒︎ **10** ☽ → ♓︎ 8:42 am *Lunar New Year (Dragon)*	
1st ♉︎ **15**	1st ♉︎ ◑ ☽ v/c 10:01 am 2nd Quarter 10:01 am ♀ → ♒︎ 11:05 am ☽ → ♊︎ 2:39 pm	2nd ♊︎ **17**	
2nd ♌︎ **22** ☽ v/c 11:18 pm	2nd ♌︎ **23** ☿ → ♓︎ 2:29 am ☽ → ♍︎ 8:38 pm	2nd ♍︎ ○ Full Moon 7:30 am *Quickening Moon*	
3rd ♏︎ **29** *Leap Day*	*1*	*2*	
7	*8*	*9*	

Aspects & Moon Phases

☌ Conjunction	0°	● New Moon	(1st Quarter)
⚹ Sextile	60°	◑ Waxing Moon	(2nd Quarter)
☐ Square	90°	○ Full Moon	(3rd Quarter)
△ Trine	120°	◐ Waning Moon	(4th Quarter)
⚻ Quincunx	150°		
☍ Opposition	180°		

MARCH 2024

SU	M	T	W
25	26	27	28
3rd ♐︎ 4th Quarter 10:23 am ◑	**4th** ♐︎ 4 ☽ v/c 10:41 am ☽ → ♑︎ 4:15 pm	**4th** ♑︎ 5	**4th** ♑︎ 6 ☽ v/c 2:35 pm ☽ → ♒︎ 7:38 pm
4th ♓︎ New Moon 5:00 am ● ☽ v/c 3:45 pm ☽ → ♈︎ 8:19 pm *Daylight Saving Time* *begins at 2:00 am* *Ramadan begins at sundown* New Moon	**1st** ♈︎ 11 ♀ → ♓︎ 5:50 pm	**1st** ♈︎ 12 ☽ v/c 7:08 am ☽ → ♉︎ 8:28 pm	**1st** ♉︎ 13
1st ♊︎ 2nd Quarter 12:11 am ◐ ☽ v/c 12:43 am ☽ → ♋︎ 5:40 am *St. Patrick's Day*	**2nd** ♋︎ 18	**2nd** ♋︎ 19 ☽ v/c 2:52 pm ☽ → ♌︎ 3:33 pm ☉ → ♈︎ 11:06 pm *Ostara* *Sun enters Aries* *Spring Equinox*	**2nd** ♌︎ 20
2nd ♍︎ 24 ☽ v/c 11:49 am ☽ → ♎︎ 4:37 pm	**2nd** ♎︎ Full Moon 3:00 am ○ *Lunar Eclipse/* *Storm Moon*	**3rd** ♎︎ 26 ☽ v/c 7:09 pm	**3rd** ♎︎ 27 ☽ → ♏︎ 5:03 am
3rd ♐︎ 31 ☽ v/c 8:16 pm *Easter*	1	2	3

Eastern Standard Time (EST) becomes Eastern Daylight Time (EDT) March 10

Zodiac Signs
♈︎ Aries	♌︎ Leo	♐︎ Sagittarius
♉︎ Taurus	♍︎ Virgo	♑︎ Capricorn
♊︎ Gemini	♎︎ Libra	♒︎ Aquarius
♋︎ Cancer	♏︎ Scorpio	♓︎ Pisces

Planets
☉ Sun	♃ Jupiter
☽ Moon	♄ Saturn
☿ Mercury	♅ Uranus
♀ Venus	♆ Neptune
♂ Mars	♇ Pluto

TH	F	SA	NOTES
29	3rd ♏ **1**	3rd ♏ **2** ☽ v/c 2:47 am ☽ → ♐ 8:56 am	
4th ♒ **7**	4th ♒ **8** ☽ v/c 1:56 pm ☽ → ♓ 8:03 pm	4th ♓ **9** ☿ → ♈ 11:03 pm	
1st ♉ **14** ☽ v/c 6:29 pm ☽ → ♊ 11:16 pm	1st ♊ **15**	1st ♊ **16**	
2nd ♌ **21**	2nd ♌ **22** ☽ v/c 2:34 am ☽ → ♍ 3:42 am ♂ → ♓ 7:47 pm	2nd ♍ **23**	
3rd ♏ **28**	3rd ♏ **29** ☽ v/c 11:40 am ☽ → ♐ 3:52 pm *Good Friday*	3rd ♐ **30**	
4	5	6	

ASPECTS & MOON PHASES

☌ Conjunction	0°	● New Moon	(1st Quarter)
✶ Sextile	60°	◐ Waxing Moon	(2nd Quarter)
□ Square	90°	○ Full Moon	(3rd Quarter)
△ Trine	120°	◑ Waning Moon	(4th Quarter)
⚻ Quincunx	150°		
☍ Opposition	180°		

APRIL 2024

SU	M	T	W
31	3rd ♐ ☽ → ♑ 12:05 am ☿ ℞ 6:14 pm 4th Quarter 11:15 pm ◗ *All Fools' Day* *Mercury retrograde*	4th ♑ 2	4th ♑ 3 ☽ v/c 1:40 am ☽ → ≈ 5:08 am
4th ♓ 7 ☽ v/c 4:27 am ☽ → ♈ 7:25 am	4th ♈ 8 New Moon 2:21 pm ● ☽ v/c 10:39 pm *Solar Eclipse/* *New Moon*	1st ♈ 9 ☽ → ♉ 7:23 am *Ramadan ends*	1st ♉ 10
1st ♋ 14	1st ♋ 15 2nd Quarter 3:13 pm ◑ ☽ v/c 7:22 pm ☽ → ♌ 10:24 pm	2nd ♌ 16	2nd ♌ 17
2nd ♎ 21	2nd ♎ 22 ☽ v/c 7:24 pm *Earth Day*	2nd ♎ 23 ☽ → ♏ 11:20 am Full Moon 7:49 pm ○ *Wind Moon*	3rd ♏ 24
3rd ♐ 28 ☽ v/c 3:31 am ☽ → ♑ 5:37 am	3rd ♑ 29 ♀ → ♉ 7:31 am	3rd ♑ 30 ☽ v/c 11:19 am ☽ → ≈ 11:20 am ♂ → ♈ 11:33 am	1
5	6	7	8

Eastern Daylight Time (EDT)

ZODIAC SIGNS

♈ Aries	♌ Leo	♐ Sagittarius
♉ Taurus	♍ Virgo	♑ Capricorn
♊ Gemini	♎ Libra	≈ Aquarius
♋ Cancer	♏ Scorpio	♓ Pisces

PLANETS

☉ Sun	♃ Jupiter
☽ Moon	♄ Saturn
☿ Mercury	♅ Uranus
♀ Venus	♆ Neptune
♂ Mars	♇ Pluto

APRIL 2024

TH	F	SA	NOTES
4 4th ♒	**5** 4th ♒ ♀ → ♈ 12:00 am ☽ v/c 1:40 am ☽ → ♓ 7:13 am	**6** 4th ♓	
11 1st ♉ ☽ v/c 6:04 am ☽ → ♊ 8:59 am	**12** 1st ♊	**13** 1st ♊ ☽ v/c 10:46 am ☽ → ♋ 1:45 pm	
18 2nd ♌ ☽ v/c 8:02 am ☽ → ♍ 10:10 am	**19** 2nd ♍ ☉ → ♉ 10:00 am *Sun enters Taurus*	**20** 2nd ♍ ☽ v/c 8:20 pm ☽ → ♎ 11:08 pm	
25 3rd ♏ ☿ D 8:54 am ☽ v/c 7:17 pm ☽ → ♐ 9:37 pm *Mercury direct*	**26** 3rd ♐	**27** 3rd ♐	
2	**3**	**4**	
9	**10**	**11**	

Aspects & Moon Phases

☌ Conjunction	0°	● New Moon	(1st Quarter)
⚹ Sextile	60°	◑ Waxing Moon	(2nd Quarter)
☐ Square	90°	○ Full Moon	(3rd Quarter)
△ Trine	120°	◐ Waning Moon	(4th Quarter)
⚻ Quincunx	150°		
☍ Opposition	180°		

MAY 2024

SU	M	T	W
28	29	30	**3rd ≈** 4th Quarter 7:27 am ◑ *Beltane*
4th ♈ 5	**4th ♈** 6 ☽ v/c 1:57 am ☽ → ♉ 5:42 pm	**4th ♉** 7 New Moon 11:22 pm ● *New Moon*	**1st ♉** 8 ☽ v/c 5:55 pm ☽ → ♊ 7:20 pm
1st ⊗ 12 *Mother's Day*	**1st ⊗** 13 ☽ v/c 5:13 am ☽ → ♌ 6:36 am	**1st ♌** 14	**1st ♌** 15 ◑ 2nd Quarter 7:48 am ☽ v/c 12:41 pm ☿ → ♉ 1:05 pm ☽ → ♍ 5:33 pm
2nd ♎ 19 ☽ v/c 11:48 am	**2nd ♎** 20 ☉ → ♊ 8:59 am ☽ → ♏ 6:34 pm *Sun enters Gemini*	**2nd ♏** 21	**2nd ♏** 22
3rd ♑ 26	**3rd ♑** 27 ☽ v/c 4:02 pm ☽ → ≈ 4:45 pm *Memorial Day*	**3rd ≈** 28	**3rd ≈** 29 ☽ v/c 10:20 am ☽ → ♓ 8:33 pm
2	3	4	5

Eastern Daylight Time (EDT)

ZODIAC SIGNS

♈ Aries	♌ Leo	♐ Sagittarius
♉ Taurus	♍ Virgo	♑ Capricorn
♊ Gemini	♎ Libra	≈ Aquarius
⊗ Cancer	♏ Scorpio	♓ Pisces

PLANETS

☉ Sun	♃ Jupiter
☽ Moon	♄ Saturn
☿ Mercury	♅ Uranus
♀ Venus	♆ Neptune
♂ Mars	♇ Pluto

TH	F	SA	NOTES
2 4th ♒︎ ☽ v/c 5:28 am ♀ ℞ 1:46 pm ☽ → ♓︎ 2:52 pm	**3** 4th ♓︎	**4** 4th ♓︎ ☽ v/c 3:06 pm ☽ → ♈︎ 4:41 pm	
9 1st ♊︎	**10** 1st ♊︎ ☽ v/c 9:49 pm ☽ → ♋︎ 11:13 pm	**11** 1st ♋︎	
16 2nd ♍︎	**17** 2nd ♍︎	**18** 2nd ♍︎ ☽ v/c 5:09 am ☽ → ♎︎ 6:23 am	
○ 2nd ♏︎ ☽ v/c 3:28 am ☽ → ♐︎ 4:24 am Full Moon 9:53 am ♀ → ♊︎ 4:30 pm *Flower Moon*	**24** 3rd ♐︎	**25** 3rd ♐︎ ☽ v/c 10:47 am ☽ → ♑︎ 11:36 am ♃ → ♊︎ 7:15 pm	
◑ 3rd ♓︎ 4th Quarter 1:13 pm	**31** 4th ♓︎ ☽ v/c 10:55 pm ☽ → ♈︎ 11:28 pm	*1*	
6	*7*	*8*	

Aspects & Moon Phases

☌ Conjunction	0°	● New Moon (1st Quarter)
✶ Sextile	60°	◐ Waxing Moon (2nd Quarter)
☐ Square	90°	○ Full Moon (3rd Quarter)
△ Trine	120°	◑ Waning Moon (4th Quarter)
⚻ Quincunx	150°	
☍ Opposition	180°	

JUNE 2024

SU	M	T	W
26	27	28	29
2 4th ♈ ☽ v/c 6:04 pm	**3** 4th ♈ ☽ → ♉ 1:55 am ☿ → ♊ 3:37 am	**4** 4th ♉	**5** 4th ♉ ☽ v/c 4:09 am ☽ → ♊ 4:36 am
9 1st ♋ ♂ → ♉ 12:35 am ☽ v/c 3:05 pm ☽ → ♌ 3:29 pm	**10** 1st ♌	**11** 1st ♌ ☽ v/c 3:16 pm	**12** 1st ♌ ☽ → ♍ 1:39 am
16 2nd ♎ Father's Day	**17** 2nd ♎ ☽ v/c 2:05 am ♀ → ♋ 2:20 am ☽ → ♏ 2:38 am ☿ → ♋ 5:07 am	**18** 2nd ♏	**19** 2nd ♏ ☽ v/c 12:19 pm ☽ → ♐ 12:32 pm Juneteenth
23 3rd ♑ ☽ v/c 11:05 pm ☽ → ♒ 11:14 pm	**24** 3rd ♒	**25** 3rd ♒ ☽ v/c 6:30 pm	**26** 3rd ♒ ☽ → ♓ 2:08 am
30 4th ♈ ☽ v/c 12:56 am ☽ → ♉ 8:00 am	1	2	3

Eastern Daylight Time (EDT)

ZODIAC SIGNS

♈ Aries	♌ Leo	♐ Sagittarius
♉ Taurus	♍ Virgo	♑ Capricorn
♊ Gemini	♎ Libra	♒ Aquarius
♋ Cancer	♏ Scorpio	♓ Pisces

PLANETS

☉ Sun	♃ Jupiter
☽ Moon	♄ Saturn
☿ Mercury	♅ Uranus
♀ Venus	♆ Neptune
♂ Mars	♇ Pluto

JUNE 2024

TH	F	SA	NOTES
30	31	4th ♈ 1	
4th ♊ ● New Moon 8:38 am *New Moon*	1st ♊ 7 ☽ v/c 8:16 am ☽ → ♋ 8:41 am	1st ♋ 8	
1st ♍ 13	1st ♍ ◐ 14 2nd Quarter 1:18 am ☽ v/c 1:54 pm ☽ → ♎ 2:12 pm	2nd ♎ 15	
2nd ♐ 20 ☉ → ♋ 4:51 pm *Litha* *Sun enters Cancer* *Summer Solstice*	2nd ♐ ○ 21 ☽ v/c 6:58 pm ☽ → ♑ 7:08 pm Full Moon 9:08 pm *Strong Sun Moon*	3rd ♑ 22	
3rd ♓ 27	3rd ♓ ◑ 28 ☽ v/c 4:45 am ☽ → ♈ 4:52 am 4th Quarter 5:53 pm	4th ♈ 29 ♄ ℞ 3:07 pm	
4	5	6	

Aspects & Moon Phases

☌ Conjunction	0°	● New Moon	(1st Quarter)
✶ Sextile	60°	◐ Waxing Moon	(2nd Quarter)
□ Square	90°	○ Full Moon	(3rd Quarter)
△ Trine	120°	◑ Waning Moon	(4th Quarter)
⚻ Quincunx	150°		
☍ Opposition	180°		

JULY 2024

SU	M	T	W
30	**1** 4th ♉	**2** 4th ♉ ♆ Rx 6:40 am ☿ → ♌ 8:50 am ☽ v/c 11:43 am ☽ → ♊ 11:50 am	**3** 4th ♊
7 1st ♌	**8** 1st ♌	**9** 1st ♌ ☽ v/c 2:04 am ☽ → ♍ 9:48 am	**10** 1st ♍
14 2nd ♎ ☽ → ♏ 10:53 am	**15** 2nd ♏	**16** 2nd ♏ ☽ v/c 9:10 pm ☽ → ♐ 9:25 pm	**17** 2nd ♐
21 2nd ♑ ○ Full Moon 6:17 am ☽ v/c 7:26 am ☽ → ♒ 7:43 am *Blessing Moon*	**22** 3rd ♒ ☉ → ♌ 3:44 am *Sun enters Leo*	**23** 3rd ♒ ☽ v/c 5:58 am ☽ → ♓ 9:23 am	**24** 3rd ♓
28 4th ♉	**29** 4th ♉ ☽ v/c 4:59 pm ☽ → ♊ 5:28 pm	**30** 4th ♊	**31** 4th ♊ ☽ v/c 10:46 pm ☽ → ♋ 11:19 pm
4	5	6	7

Eastern Daylight Time (EDT)

ZODIAC SIGNS

♈ Aries   ♌ Leo   ♐ Sagittarius
♉ Taurus   ♍ Virgo   ♑ Capricorn
♊ Gemini   ♎ Libra   ♒ Aquarius
♋ Cancer   ♏ Scorpio   ♓ Pisces

PLANETS

☉ Sun   ♃ Jupiter
☽ Moon   ♄ Saturn
☿ Mercury   ♅ Uranus
♀ Venus   ♆ Neptune
♂ Mars   ♇ Pluto

JULY 2024

TH	F	SA	NOTES
4 4th ♊ ☽ v/c 4:44 pm ☽ → ♋ 4:51 pm *Independence Day*	4th ♋ ● New Moon 6:57 pm *New Moon*	**6** 1st ♋ ☽ v/c 11:47 pm ☽ → ♌ 11:56 pm	
11 1st ♍ ♀ → ♌ 12:19 pm ☽ v/c 9:55 pm ☽ → ♎ 10:06 pm	**12** 1st ♎	1st ♎ ◗ ☽ v/c 6:49 pm 2nd Quarter 6:49 pm	
18 2nd ♐	**19** 2nd ♐ ☽ v/c 3:58 am ☽ → ♑ 4:14 am	**20** 2nd ♑ ♂ → ♊ 4:43 pm	
25 3rd ♓ ☽ v/c 10:31 am ☽ → ♈ 10:52 am ☿ → ♍ 6:42 pm	**26** 3rd ♈ ☽ v/c 6:14 pm	3rd ♈ ◑ ☽ → ♉ 1:23 pm 4th Quarter 10:52 pm	
1	2	3	
8	9	10	

Aspects & Moon Phases

♂ Conjunction	0°	● New Moon	(1st Quarter)
✳ Sextile	60°	◗ Waxing Moon	(2nd Quarter)
☐ Square	90°	○ Full Moon	(3rd Quarter)
△ Trine	120°	◖ Waning Moon	(4th Quarter)
⚼ Quincunx	150°		
☍ Opposition	180°		

AUGUST 2024

SU	M	T	W
28	29	30	31
4th ♌ New Moon 7:13 am ♀ → ♍ 10:23 pm ● *New Moon*	1st ♌ **5** ☿ ℞ 12:56 am ☽ v/c 11:16 am ☽ → ♍ 5:17 pm *Mercury retrograde*	1st ♍ **6**	1st ♍ **7**
1st ♏ **11**	1st ♏ **12** ◐ 2nd Quarter 11:19 am	2nd ♏ **13** ☽ v/c 5:01 am ☽ → ♐ 6:01 am	2nd ♐ **14** ☿ → ♌ 8:16 pm
2nd ♒ **18**	2nd ♒ **19** ○ ☽ v/c 2:26 pm Full Moon 2:26 pm ☽ → ♓ 6:52 pm *Corn Moon*	3rd ♓ **20**	3rd ♓ **21** ☽ v/c 5:54 pm ☽ → ♈ 7:02 pm
3rd ♉ **25** ☽ v/c 9:40 pm ☽ → ♊ 11:04 pm	3rd ♊ **26** ◑ 4th Quarter 5:26 am	4th ♊ **27**	4th ♊ **28** ☽ v/c 3:14 am ☽ → ♋ 4:47 am ☿ D 5:14 pm *Mercury direct*
1	2	3	4

Eastern Daylight Time (EDT)

ZODIAC SIGNS

♈ Aries	♌ Leo	♐ Sagittarius
♉ Taurus	♍ Virgo	♑ Capricorn
♊ Gemini	♎ Libra	♒ Aquarius
♋ Cancer	♏ Scorpio	♓ Pisces

PLANETS

☉ Sun	♃ Jupiter
☽ Moon	♄ Saturn
☿ Mercury	♅ Uranus
♀ Venus	♆ Neptune
♂ Mars	♇ Pluto

AUGUST 2024

TH	F	SA	NOTES
4th ⊛ **1** *Lammas*	4th ⊛ **2**	4th ⊛ **3** ☽ v/c 6:31 am ☽ → ♌ 7:10 am	
1st ♍ **8** ☽ v/c 4:40 am ☽ → ♎ 5:31 am	1st ♎ **9** ☽ v/c 5:45 pm	1st ♎ **10** ☽ → ♏ 6:34 pm	
2nd ♐ **15** ☽ v/c 12:52 pm ☽ → ♑ 1:51 pm	2nd ♑ **16**	2nd ♑ **17** ☽ v/c 4:43 pm ☽ → ♒ 5:45 pm	
3rd ♈ **22** ☉ → ♍ 10:55 am *Sun enters Virgo*	3rd ♈ **23** ☽ v/c 8:44 am ☽ → ♉ 8:00 pm	3rd ♉ **24**	
4th ⊛ **29** ♀ → ♎ 9:23 am	4th ⊛ **30** ☽ v/c 11:24 am ☽ → ♌ 1:09 pm	4th ♌ **31**	
5	*6*	*7*	

ASPECTS & MOON PHASES

☌ Conjunction	0°	● New Moon	(1st Quarter)
✶ Sextile	60°	◐ Waxing Moon	(2nd Quarter)
☐ Square	90°	○ Full Moon	(3rd Quarter)
△ Trine	120°	◑ Waning Moon	(4th Quarter)
⚻ Quincunx	150°		
☍ Opposition	180°		

SEPTEMBER 2024

SU	M	T	W
1 4th ♌ ♅ R̥ 11:18 am ♀ → ♑ 8:10 pm ☽ v/c 8:25 pm ☽ → ♍ 11:48 pm 4th ♍	New Moon 9:56 pm ● *New Moon* *Labor Day*	**3** 1st ♍	**4** 1st ♍ ☽ v/c 12:06 pm ☽ → ♎ 12:12 pm ♂ → ♋ 3:46 pm
8 1st ♏	**9** 1st ♏ ☿ → ♍ 2:50 am ☽ v/c 1:11 pm ☽ → ♐ 1:26 pm	**10** 1st ♐	**11** 1st ♐ ◑ 2nd Quarter 2:06 am ☽ v/c 8:21 pm ☽ → ♑ 10:38 pm
15 2nd ♒	**16** 2nd ♒ ☽ v/c 1:04 am ☽ → ♓ 5:39 am	**17** 2nd ♓ ○ Full Moon 10:34 pm *Lunar Eclipse/* *Harvest Moon*	**18** 3rd ♓ ☽ v/c 5:02 am ☽ → ♈ 5:24 am
22 3rd ♉ ☽ v/c 6:14 am ☽ → ♊ 6:24 am ☉ → ♎ 8:44 am ♀ → ♏ 10:36 pm *Mabon* *Sun enters Libra* *Fall Equinox*	**23** 3rd ♊	**24** 3rd ♊ ◐ ☽ v/c 7:59 am ☽ → ♋ 10:50 am 4th Quarter 2:50 pm	**25** 4th ♋
29 4th ♌ ☽ → ♍ 5:42 am	**30** 4th ♍	*1*	*2*
6	*7*	*8*	*9*

Eastern Daylight Time (EDT)

ZODIAC SIGNS

♈ Aries   ♌ Leo   ♐ Sagittarius
♉ Taurus   ♍ Virgo   ♑ Capricorn
♊ Gemini   ♎ Libra   ♒ Aquarius
♋ Cancer   ♏ Scorpio   ♓ Pisces

PLANETS

☉ Sun   ♃ Jupiter
☽ Moon   ♄ Saturn
☿ Mercury   ♅ Uranus
♀ Venus   ♆ Neptune
♂ Mars   ♇ Pluto

SEPTEMBER 2024

TH	F	SA	NOTES
1st ♎ **5**	1st ♎ **6**	1st ♎ **7** ☽ v/c 1:08 am ☽ → ♏ 1:18 am	
2nd ♑ **12**	2nd ♑ **13**	2nd ♑ **14** ☽ v/c 3:35 am ☽ → ♒ 3:53 am	
3rd ♈ **19**	3rd ♈ **20** ☽ v/c 4:39 am ☽ → ♉ 5:03 am	3rd ♉ **21**	
4th ♋ **26** ☿ → ♎ 4:09 am ☽ v/c 6:12 pm ☽ → ♌ 6:47 pm	4th ♌ **27**	4th ♌ **28** ☽ v/c 11:36 pm	
3	**4**	**5**	
10	**11**	**12**	

Aspects & Moon Phases

☌ Conjunction	0°	● New Moon	(1st Quarter)
⚹ Sextile	60°	◐ Waxing Moon	(2nd Quarter)
☐ Square	90°	○ Full Moon	(3rd Quarter)
△ Trine	120°	◑ Waning Moon	(4th Quarter)
⚻ Quincunx	150°		
☍ Opposition	180°		

OCTOBER 2024

SU	M	T	W
29	30	**1** 4th ♍ ☽ v/c 5:39 pm ☽ → ♎ 6:20 pm	**1** 4th ♎ New Moon 2:49 ● *Solar Eclipse/New Moon*
6 1st ♏ ☽ v/c 6:52 pm ☽ → ♐ 7:34 pm	**7** 1st ♐	**8** 1st ♐	**9** 1st ♐ ☽ v/c 1:54 am ♃ ℞ 3:05 am ☽ → ♑ 5:38 am
13 2nd ♒ ☽ v/c 10:11 am ☿ → ♏ 3:23 pm ☽ → ♓ 3:55 pm	**14** 2nd ♓	**15** 2nd ♓ ☽ v/c 4:00 pm ☽ → ♈ 4:34 pm	**16** 2nd ♈
20 3rd ♊	**21** 3rd ♊ ☽ v/c 5:00 pm ☽ → ♋ 6:50 pm	**22** 3rd ♋ ☉ → ♏ 6:15 pm *Sun enters Scorpio*	**23** 3rd ♋
27 4th ♍	**28** 4th ♍ ☽ v/c 11:54 pm	**29** 4th ♍ ☽ → ♎ 12:30 am	**30** 4th ♎
3	4	5	6

Eastern Daylight Time (EDT)

ZODIAC SIGNS

♈ Aries	♌ Leo	♐ Sagittarius
♉ Taurus	♍ Virgo	♑ Capricorn
♊ Gemini	♎ Libra	♒ Aquarius
♋ Cancer	♏ Scorpio	♓ Pisces

PLANETS

☉ Sun	♃ Jupiter
☽ Moon	♄ Saturn
☿ Mercury	♅ Uranus
♀ Venus	♆ Neptune
♂ Mars	♇ Pluto

OCTOBER 2024

TH	F	SA	NOTES
1st ♎︎ **3**	1st ♎︎ **4** ☽ v/c 6:40 am ☽ → ♏︎ 7:22 am	1st ♏︎ **5**	
1st ♑︎ ◐ 2nd Quarter 2:55 pm	2nd ♑︎ **11** ☽ v/c 11:53 am ☽ → ♒︎ 12:31 pm ☿ D 8:34 pm	2nd ♒︎ **12**	
2nd ♈︎ ○ Full Moon 7:26 am ☽ v/c 3:26 pm ♀ → ♐︎ 3:28 pm ☽ → ♉︎ 4:00 pm *Blood Moon*	3rd ♉︎ **18**	3rd ♉︎ **19** ☽ v/c 3:33 pm ☽ → ♊︎ 4:07 pm	
3rd ♋︎ ◑ ☽ v/c 12:47 am ☽ → ♌︎ 1:24 am 4th Quarter 4:03 am	4th ♌︎ **25**	4th ♌︎ **26** ☽ v/c 4:04 am ☽ → ♍︎ 11:47 am	
4th ♎︎ **31** ☽ v/c 12:57 pm ☽ → ♏︎ 1:29 pm *Samhain* *Halloween*	1	2	
7	8	9	

Aspects & Moon Phases

☌ Conjunction	0°	● New Moon	(1st Quarter)
✶ Sextile	60°	◐ Waxing Moon	(2nd Quarter)
☐ Square	90°	○ Full Moon	(3rd Quarter)
△ Trine	120°	◑ Waning Moon	(4th Quarter)
⚻ Quincunx	150°		
☍ Opposition	180°		

NOVEMBER 2024

SU	M	T	W
27	28	29	30
3 1st ♏︎ ☽ v/c 12:51 am ☽ → ♐︎ 1:19 am ♂ → ♌︎ 11:10 pm *Daylight Saving Time* *ends at 2:00 am*	**4** 1st ♐︎	**5** 1st ♐︎ ☽ v/c 5:23 am ☽ → ♑︎ 10:17 am *Election Day (general)*	**6** 1st ♑︎
10 2nd ♓︎	**11** 2nd ♓︎ ♀ → ♑︎ 1:26 pm *Veterans Day*	**12** 2nd ♓︎ ☽ v/c 1:13 am ☽ → ♈︎ 1:26 am	**13** 2nd ♈︎
17 3rd ♊︎ ☽ v/c 11:09 pm	**18** 3rd ♊︎ ☽ → ♋︎ 3:50 am	**19** 3rd ♋︎ ♀ → ♒︎ 3:29 pm	**20** 3rd ♋︎ ☽ v/c 6:20 am ☽ → ♌︎ 8:51 am
24 4th ♍︎	**25** 4th ♍︎ ☽ v/c 12:35 am ☽ → ♎︎ 6:20 am ☿ ℞ 9:42 pm *Mercury retrograde*	**26** 4th ♎︎	**27** 4th ♎︎ ☽ v/c 4:14 am ☽ → ♏︎ 7:21 pm
1	2	3	4

Eastern Daylight Time (EDT) becomes Eastern Standard Time (EST) November 3

ZODIAC SIGNS

♈︎ Aries	♌︎ Leo	♐︎ Sagittarius
♉︎ Taurus	♍︎ Virgo	♑︎ Capricorn
♊︎ Gemini	♎︎ Libra	♒︎ Aquarius
♋︎ Cancer	♏︎ Scorpio	♓︎ Pisces

PLANETS

☉ Sun	♃ Jupiter
☽ Moon	♄ Saturn
☿ Mercury	♅ Uranus
♀ Venus	♆ Neptune
♂ Mars	♇ Pluto

NOVEMBER 2024

TH	F	SA	NOTES
31	4th ♏︎ **New Moon 8:47 am** ●	1st ♏︎ 2 ☿ → ♐︎ 3:18 pm	
	New Moon		
1st ♑︎ 7 ☽ v/c 5:38 pm ☽ → ♒︎ 5:58 pm	1st ♒︎ 8	1st ♒︎ ◗ 2nd Quarter 12:55 am ☽ v/c 7:23 pm ☽ → ♓︎ 11:00 pm	
2nd ♈︎ 14 ☽ v/c 1:50 am ☽ → ♉︎ 1:59 am	2nd ♉︎ ○ ♄ D 9:20 am Full Moon 4:28 pm	3rd ♉︎ 16 ☽ v/c 2:03 am ☽ → ♊︎ 2:09 am	
	Mourning Moon		
3rd ♌︎ 21 ⊙ → ♐︎ 2:56 pm	3rd ♌︎ ◗ ☽ v/c 8:15 am ☽ → ♍︎ 6:01 pm 4th Quarter 8:28 pm	4th ♍︎ 23	
Sun enters Sagittarius			
4th ♏︎ 28	4th ♏︎ 29	4th ♏︎ 30 ☽ v/c 1:19 am ☽ → ♐︎ 6:53 am	
Thanksgiving Day			
5	6	7	

ASPECTS & MOON PHASES

☌ Conjunction	0°	● New Moon	(1st Quarter)	
⚹ Sextile	60°	◐ Waxing Moon	(2nd Quarter)	
☐ Square	90°	○ Full Moon	(3rd Quarter)	
△ Trine	120°	◑ Waning Moon	(4th Quarter)	
⚻ Quincunx	150°			
☍ Opposition	180°			

DECEMBER 2024

SU	M	T	W
4th ♐ New Moon 1:21 am ● New Moon	1st ♐ 2 ☽ v/c 10:47 am ☽ → ♑ 4:09 pm	1st ♑ 3	1st ♑ 4 ☽ v/c 6:34 pm ☽ → ♒ 11:21 pm
1st ♓ 2nd Quarter 10:27 am ◑	2nd ♓ 9 ☽ v/c 3:45 am ☽ → ♈ 8:38 am	2nd ♈ 10 ☽ v/c 5:13 pm	2nd ♈ 11 ☽ → ♉ 10:55 am
2nd ♊ Full Moon 4:02 am ○ ☽ v/c 9:32 am ☽ → ♋ 2:21 pm ☿ D 3:56 pm Long Nights Moon Mercury direct	3rd ♋ 16	3rd ♋ 17 ☽ v/c 1:33 pm ☽ → ♌ 6:39 pm	3rd ♌ 18
3rd ♍ ◐ ☽ v/c 8:27 am ☽ → ♎ 2:08 pm 4th Quarter 5:18 pm	4th ♎ 23	4th ♎ 24 ☽ v/c 5:44 am Christmas Eve	4th ♎ 25 ☽ → ♏ 3:06 am Christmas Day Hanukkah begins at sundown (ends Jan. 2)
4th ♐ 29 ☽ v/c 6:34 pm ☽ → ♑ 11:37 pm	4th ♑ New Moon 5:27 pm ● New Moon	1st ♑ 31 New Year's Eve	I
5	6	7	8

Eastern Standard Time (EST)

ZODIAC SIGNS

♈ Aries	♌ Leo	♐ Sagittarius
♉ Taurus	♍ Virgo	♑ Capricorn
♊ Gemini	♎ Libra	♒ Aquarius
♋ Cancer	♏ Scorpio	♓ Pisces

PLANETS

☉ Sun	♃ Jupiter
☽ Moon	♄ Saturn
☿ Mercury	♅ Uranus
♀ Venus	♆ Neptune
♂ Mars	♇ Pluto

DECEMBER 2024

TH	F	SA	NOTES
1st ♒ **5**	1st ♒ **6** ♂ ℞ 6:33 pm ☽ v/c 7:01 pm *Mars retrograde*	1st ♒ **7** ♀ → ♒ 1:13 am ☽ → ♓ 4:49 am ♆ D 6:43 pm	
2nd ♉ **12**	2nd ♉ **13** ☽ v/c 7:39 am ☽ → ♊ 12:22 pm	2nd ♊ **14**	
3rd ♌ **19**	3rd ♌ **20** ☽ v/c 12:19 am ☽ → ♍ 2:37 am	3rd ♍ **21** ☉ → ♑ 4:21 am *Yule* *Sun enters Capricorn* *Winter Solstice*	
4th ♏ **26** *Kwanzaa begins (ends Jan. 1)*	4th ♏ **27** ☽ v/c 9:24 am ☽ → ♐ 2:46 pm	4th ♐ **28**	
2	**3**	**4**	
9	**10**	**11**	

ASPECTS & MOON PHASES

♂ Conjunction	0°	● New Moon	(1st Quarter)
✶ Sextile	60°	◑ Waxing Moon	(2nd Quarter)
☐ Square	90°	○ Full Moon	(3rd Quarter)
△ Trine	120°	◑ Waning Moon	(4th Quarter)
⚼ Quincunx	150°		
☍ Opposition	180°